The process of asking for, receiving & giving

LOVE &FORGIVENESS

The process of asking for, receiving & giving

LOVE &FORGIVENESS

LaShawnda Jones

Jazzy Media LLC
New York

The Process of Asking for, Receiving & Giving Love and Forgiveness. Copyright © 2011 by LaShawnda Jones. All rights reserved. Jazzy Media LLC Printed in the United States of America. No part of this book may be used or reproduced in any manner whatsoever without written permission except in the case of brief quotations embodied in critical articles and reviews. For more information, please visit **www.mygodandme.info** or write to **lashawnda.jones@mygodandme.info**.

Unless otherwise indicated, all *Old Testament* and *New Testament* scripture quotations are taken from the New Living Translation version on **www.Bible.com**, © 1995 Bible.com Ministries, Dewey, Arizona.

All word definitions are taken from **www.Dictionary.com** *Unabridged (v 1.1)*, Based on the Random House Unabridged Dictionary, © Random House, Inc. 2006.

Author photo by Jadon Good
Cover design by Katie Drapp
Edited by Cory Bilicko

Category: Christian Living, Relationships– Inspiration & Personal Growth

First edition. ISBN: 978-0-9776179-9-9

To my husband, whom God is preparing for me and for whom I am being prepared. Together, may we always stand on and move according to the Word of God. Loving each other and learning and growing through our union in this life.

Other books by LaShawnda Jones

My God and Me: Listening, Learning and Growing on My Journey
(Jazzy Media LLC)

Contributor
Go, Tell Michelle: African American Women
Write to the New First Lady
(Excelsior Editions)
Compiled and Edited by
Barbara A. Seals Nevergold and Peggy Brooks-Bertram

Available at:
www.mygodandme.info
www.amazon.com
www.bn.com

Please note: The experiences noted in this book are from the author's perspective and understanding. This book is meant to be a tool for Bible study on the topics presented.

God bless you,

LaShawnda

Contents

Introduction
You Must Believe to Understand … 11

Love
Worldly "Love" Lesson … 19
I Want to Know What Love Is … 20
What is Love? … 21
Show Me the Love … 28
I Love You, but God Loves You More … 35
Are You Ready for Love? … 42
First Fruits of All Your Crops … 47
What Makes You Happy? … 57
Power of Love … 60
When Your Love is Rejected … 62

Repentance
What does it mean to "repent"? … 69
Psalm 51 … 72
The Psalm 51 Example: Repent & Live … 74

Why Repent?	82
Repentance Leads to Healing	84
The Benefit of Repentance	90
The Importance of Repentance	94
Dealing with the Unrepentant	97
You've Repented. Now What?	100
The Relationship Between Repentance & Forgiveness	102

Forgiveness

The Magnitude of Forgiveness	109
Forgiveness Does the Body Good	119
Question: To Forgive or Not to Forgive?	129
You Forgave. Now What?	136
Negotiating Forgiveness for a Better Relationship	138

Communication

The "Ask, Receive, Give" Process Explained	147
Importance of Communication	149
Failure to Communicate	154
Self-Communication	161

Pop Culture vs. The Bible

Led Astray by Pop Culture	167

Oneness of Giving and Receiving

Oneness	175
The Difference Between Believers & Nonbelievers	178
Acceptance is Crucial	183
Duality of Man: Strength & Vulnerability	188

Scripture Index   197

Introduction
You Must Believe to Understand

> [F]or you are a chosen people. You are royal priests, a holy nation, God's very own possession. As a result, you can show others the goodness of God, for he called you out of the darkness into his wonderful light. Dear friends, I warn you as "temporary residents and foreigners" to keep away from worldly desires that wage war against your very souls. Be careful to live properly among your unbelieving neighbors. Then even if they accuse you of doing wrong, they will see your honorable behavior, and they will give honor to God when he judges the world.
> 1 Peter 2:9, 11-12

The most difficult tasks involved in writing *The Process of Asking for, Receiving and Giving Love and Forgiveness* were deciding to whom to address the text and to maintain that focus throughout the book.

My questions to "self" consisted of: Am I writing to the people who love, or to the people who are loved? Am I addressing the repentant at heart, or the unrepentant? Should I focus on those who have forgiven, or those who have received forgiveness? Is this work ultimately for people who believe in God, His Son Jesus and His Holy Spirit, or for those who don't believe at all?

The answer from "self" was: everyone represents, has represented or will represent each of those characteristics at any given point of their life.

This book is a tool to be used in working out love, repentance and forgiveness issues in human relationships through the examples God has provided. Those relationships could be with parents, siblings, spouses, other family members, friends, co-workers, neighbors or community members. There are many relationships during the course of our lives through which we have to navigate our way. Some of those relationships fail and die because one or both parties involved are unfamiliar with the process of love, repentance and forgiveness. Love, repentance and forgiveness are more than just words that you speak and forget about. Love requires action. Repenting mends the love you hurt. Forgiveness is a loving response to the attack on love. They are all choices. Asking is involved. Receiving is necessary. Giving is the only way each is shared.

The Process of Asking for, Receiving and Giving Love and Forgiveness is a work by a Christian woman who has chosen to purposefully sow into the Kingdom of Heaven. My goal with this book is to speak directly to *anyone* with eyes, ears and a heart open to see, hear and receive the truth of the Word of God. The majority of Biblical scripture used in this volume is addressed to Believers from the mouths and pens of Jesus and His Disciples.

The Holy Bible is a Teacher's Manual full of instructions telling Believers (*a.k.a.* Teacher Aides) how to conduct themselves... and how to show God to other people. Believers are commissioned to teach the world by showing nonbelievers God's ways through their mode of living and their treatment of others. The Father's process is very deliberate!

> *The Lord isn't really being slow about his promise, as some people think. No, he is being patient for your sake. He does not want anyone to be destroyed, but wants everyone to repent.*
>
> *~ 2 Peter 3:9-10*

This knowledge encouraged me to address Believers and nonbelievers alike. My hope is that the Believer will be encouraged, edified and strengthened; and that the nonbeliever will be exposed to a truth they can no longer deny and will begin to pursue.

What does it mean to "believe"?

God's word is locked. His secrets are hidden. His word does not make sense to everyone. He does not reveal knowledge and understanding to all of Creation. But those He call His children are permitted to know His secrets and understand His ways through His Spirit.

How do you become a Child of God?

You must believe on and receive the One He sent – Jesus Christ the Messiah.

We must have confidence in and be convicted of God's existence. That's how we believe. By believing in His existence, we can then believe in His works.

> *He came into the very world he created, but the world didn't recognize Him. He came to his own people, and even they rejected Him. But to all who believed Him and accepted Him, He gave the right to become children of God. They are reborn — not with a physical birth resulting from human passion or plan, but a birth that comes from God.*
>
> *~ John 1:10-12*

Having faith is another way of expressing belief in God. *Hebrews 11:1* tells us that faith is the confidence that our hopes will manifest and it assures us about the things we cannot see. *Hebrews 11:6* further explains:

> *And without faith it is impossible to please God, because anyone who comes to Him must believe that He exists and that He rewards those who earnestly seek Him.*

Again, this may not make sense to a nonbeliever, but then again a nonbeliever wouldn't be reading this if they weren't seeking truth. So, if that's you, keep on reading!

For the Believers, this may be elementary, but a review never hurts anyone. So, you keep reading as well!

Do you believe God?

You acknowledge that God exists, but do you have enough confidence in His existence to obey His Word? To believe God is to accept what He says as true. He doesn't allow picking and choosing or alternating between a straight walk and a zigzag. If you claim to believe *in* God, but you do not believe *what He says* in the Bible (His Word), then you do not really *believe* God. God and His Word are one. "The Word" is also another name for Jesus Christ. God and Jesus are one. If you believe God, you will believe and obey His Word. If you do not believe what God says directly or through Jesus, it is God Himself you are disbelieving and rejecting. (Yoonu Njub, 1998)

> *But these are written so that you may continue to believe that Jesus is the Messiah, the Son of God, and that by believing in Him you will have life by the power of His name.*
>
> ~ *John 20:31*

How to become a Believer

If you desire to become a child of God, a Believer, one of God's chosen people, a member of His royal priesthood and holy nation, then simply do so. All that is required is that you follow His instructions. If you desire to become one of God's very own possessions and heed His call by walking out of the darkness of the world and into His wonderful eternal light, then you have only to believe in your heart and speak with your lips the words of *Romans 10:9-10*, and ask the Father to be your Teacher and Guide for everything He wishes for you to learn on your spiritual walk with Him.

> *If you confess with your mouth that Jesus is Lord and believe in your heart that God raised Him from the dead, you will be saved. For it is by believing in your heart that you are made right with God, and it is by confessing with your mouth that you are saved. As the Scriptures tell us, "Anyone who trusts in Him will never be disgraced." Jew and Gentile are the same in this respect. They have the same Lord, who gives generously to all who call on Him. For "Everyone who calls on the name of the LORD will be saved."*
>
> *~ Romans 10:9-13*

"'You must love the LORD your God with all your heart,
all your soul, and all your mind.' This is the first and
greatest commandment. A second is equally important:
'Love your neighbor as yourself.' The entire law and all
the demands of the prophets are based on these two
commandments."
Matthew 22:37-40

Worldly "Love" Lesson

Dear friends, do not believe everyone who claims to speak by the Spirit. You must test them to see if the spirit they have comes from God. For there are many false prophets in the world. This is how we know if they have the Spirit of God: If a person claiming to be a prophet acknowledges that Jesus Christ came in a real body, that person has the Spirit of God. But if someone claims to be a prophet and does not acknowledge the truth about Jesus, that person is not from God. Such a person has the spirit of the Antichrist, which you heard is coming into the world and indeed is already here.
1 John 4:1-3

Everything I learned about love from the world: "Love" was something people claimed they had for me right before, after and/or during an act that hurt me, betrayed our relationship or devalued me as a person.

I Want to Know What Love Is

In my life there's been heartache and pain
I don't know if I can face it again
Can't stop now, I've traveled so far
To change this lonely life

I wanna know what love is
I want you to show me
I wanna feel what love is
I know you can show me

I'm gonna take a little time
A little time to look around me
I've got nowhere left to hide
It looks like love has finally found me

From the album *Agent Provocateur*
Performed by Foreigner
(Mick Jones, 1984)

What is Love?

So the LORD must wait for you to come to Him so He can show you His love and compassion.
Isaiah 30:18

You're looking for love, aren't you? If not now, you have. If you haven't, you will. It's embedded in our DNA. Who we are. We're wired to not only want love, but to need it and crave it in such a profound way that we search for it. Sometimes we spend our lives searching for it. Eventually, hopefully, we're able to seize it. Or more apropos, *Love* seizes us. Love is calling to us. Love created us. Love releases us only to see if we will return on our own. Willingly. To accept all that Love is. Amazingly, *Love* wants to be loved back.

I wanna know what love is...
In order to understand what I'm about to share with you, you need to let go of all the negative ideas you have about love. Or at least push those thoughts out of your mind while you're reading this book. You need to forget about the person who claimed to love you yet mistreated, ignored, abused, hurt or abandoned you. Dig up what they planted into your life in the name of love and toss it out of you. Those people weren't carriers of love. Bitterness, anger, hatred, jealousy, pain, frustration, manipulation, resentment, and fear are not expressions of love. Love cannot reside in the same

space as those negative characteristics. So, forget about the people who showed you those things. Empty your mind of your heartache. Empty your heart of your pain. Free yourself of your expectations. Of your frustrations. Of your dreams and secret fantasies. Let all that go. Free yourself from everything and everybody who misrepresented love to you. Take a deep breath. Pause for a moment before reading on.

Is your mind clear?

Take another deep breath.

Is your heart ready to receive?

Society tells us there are different kinds of love. That's not true. There is only one love. That one love manifests itself in many ways, none of which will harm you. Love edifies. It grows. It builds. It nurtures.

God *is* love.

That's it. That's all. Receiving those three words as ultimate truth changed my life. Since receiving those words, I've had to work backwards to dig up the misrepresentations I took as truth throughout my life. The daddy who molested me. The mother who stood by him. The friends who were jealous of me. The employers who attempted to indenture me. The romantic interests who took me for granted. They all claimed to love me – loved having me around, loved what I brought to their lives, loved how I made them feel. If I took them at their word, "love" would be such a horrible, ugly, destructive, dishonorable thing. But even before I came to know God as *Love*, I fought against what people of the world were trying to tell me *love* is. I believe you're reading this because you're fighting against what the world is telling you love is, as well.

> *Dear friends, let us continue to love one another, for love comes from God. Anyone who loves is a child of*

> God and knows God. But anyone who does not love does not know God, for God is love.
> ~ *1 John 4:7-8*

God is love.

So simple, yet life altering. In His infinite wisdom, our Creator God defines love for us in *1 Corinthians 13:4-7*

> *Love is patient and kind.*
> *Love is not jealous or boastful or proud or rude.*
> *It does not demand its own way.*
> *It is not irritable, and it keeps no record of being wronged.*
> *It does not rejoice about injustice but rejoices whenever the truth wins out.*
> *Love never gives up.*
> *It never loses faith.*
> *It is always hopeful.*
> *Love endures through every circumstance.*

God is the embodiment of all these characteristics. He is patient and kind. He will never give up on you. He will never leave you or abandon you. With Him you can survive anything the world throws at you. God's characteristics are also instructions on how we are to express love to one another. We should be patient and kind. We should not be proud or jealous or rude. We should not insist on our own way. We should be forgiving, faithful and hopeful through everything.

The only true love is God's love. Everything else is an imposter. Anything else is a lie. When we accept God for all He is, His love pours into us, flows through us and shines out from us for others to see and experience. When we truly surrender to God we are able to love others as He loves us. That's what He is looking for. We show our love for our Heavenly Father by obeying His instructions. Isn't that a wonderful circle? It's almost like recycling love. The Original Being loves us so we can love others. The act of giving love to others is showing love to God. It's an intertwined unending cycle – He never runs out of His good, invigorating, amazing love!

I wanna feel what love is

> *In peace I will lie down and sleep, for you alone, O LORD, will keep me safe.*
>
> *~ Psalm 4:8*

In the simplest terms, experiencing love results in a sense of hope, peace and security. When you feel completely secure and are at peace with yourself, no matter what is going on around you, then you are experiencing love. You're resting in the hope that all is as it should be and will only get better.

The *Book of Jeremiah* is one of my favorite books in the Old Testament. Jeremiah is the first person I put myself in place of while reading scripture. The words God spoke to him in *Jeremiah 1:5* felt as if He were speaking directly to me:

> *"I knew you before I formed you in your mother's womb. Before you were born I set you apart and appointed you as my prophet to the nations."*

What can possibly feel more secure than a mother's womb? Where else in life do we ever feel completely enveloped in love? But God knew us before He formed us and put us there. Imagine! He created that secure space for us! That love nest. That peaceful haven!

Later, God spoke through Jeremiah to the Israelites in exile in Babylon:

> "I know the plans I have for you; they are plans for good and not for disaster, to give you a future and a hope."
>
> ~ Jeremiah 29:11

Translation: *Don't despair! It looks bad, but not really because the great I AM is in control!*

That's His message. No matter what, stay secure in Him. When you rest secure in the LORD, peace is right there with you. *Psalm 91 says it best:*

> *Those who live in the shelter of the Most High will find rest in the shadow of the Almighty. This I declare about the LORD: He alone is my refuge, my place of safety; He is my God, and I trust Him. For He will rescue you from every trap, protect you from deadly disease. He will cover you with His feathers. He will shelter you with His wings. His faithful promises are your armor and protection. Do not be afraid of the terrors of the night, nor the arrow that flies in the day.*
>
> *Do not dread the disease that stalks in darkness, nor the disaster that strikes at midday. Though a thousand fall at your side, though ten thousand are dying around you, these evils will not touch you. Just open your eyes, and see how the wicked are punished.*
>
> *If you make the LORD your refuge, if you make the Most High your shelter, no evil will conquer you; no plague will come near your home. For He will order His angels to protect you wherever you go. They will hold you up with their hands so you won't even hurt your foot on a stone. You will trample upon lions and cobras; you will crush fierce lions and serpents under your feet!*
>
> *The LORD says, "I will rescue those who love me. I will protect those who trust in my name. When they*

call on me, I will answer; I will be with them in trouble. I will rescue and honor them. I will reward them with a long life and give them my salvation."

Praise God! I hope you got that! Those are promises! Guarantees from the LORD Almighty! From the Most High. From our Father in Heaven. He assures those who love Him and trust in Him that they will be rescued from all they encounter. Their reward is salvation and long life in Him.

Translation: *Security, peace and hope.* We already have it. We just have to seize it.

I want you to show me...

Love is an action. Love is something you do, give and show. You can feel it and see it too, but only in the process of *doing* and *giving* are you *showing* love. We need to be representatives and exhibitors of love. People speak of love all the time, but if they aren't showing love, they don't know what they're talking about. If they can't speak of God as love, they are sincerely clueless.

In *Galatians 5:22-23* we are told what the Spirit of God in us produces in our life.

> *But the Holy Spirit produces this kind of fruit in our lives: love, joy, peace, patience, kindness, goodness, faithfulness, gentleness, and self-control.*

In other words, when we recognize and acknowledge that God is in us – His Loving Holy Spirit lives within us – these characteristics will be evident in our lives. These are the characteristics we have to show to other people as representatives of our Lord. It doesn't matter who the other people are or what they believe. "Other people" do not determine how a Believer applies his or her beliefs in their life. After all, the Believer will be judged, at the end, based on their own behavior, not others' behavior towards them.

Show Me the Love

> *Dear children, let's not merely say that we love each other; let us show the truth by our actions. Our actions will show that we belong to the truth, so we will be confident when we stand before God.*
> *1 John 3:18-19*

> *Then the LORD said to me, "Go and love your wife again, even though she commits adultery with another lover. This will illustrate that the LORD still loves Israel, even though the people have turned to other gods and love to worship them."*
> *Hosea 3:1*

Occasionally, I have to remind people that I am a work in progress, just like them. Though I continue to strive, I have not reached the mark *(Philippians 3:12-14)*, just like you. When I first read God's instruction to Hosea, I was taken aback. I felt sorry for Hosea. Goodness, to be explicitly instructed to take an adulterous spouse back! That couldn't be me! Oh, no!

But, it is me. It is all of us, isn't it? We have all violated the trust, love, loyalty, and faithfulness of someone near and dear to us. Mother, father, brother, sister, husband, wife, friend. And our sentiments have also been violated by one or many of them also. We have all fallen short of perfection in our relationships. If we were all perfect, what would be the purpose of this life?

Everything we go through in life is for our perfecting, for our improvement, for our growth. I've come to see God's instruction to Hosea as God's instruction to me in working through the hurts received during my interactions with people. *LaShawnda, go show your love to _____, though they set you aside for someone else (betrayed, neglected, ignored or disregarded you). Love _____ as the Lord loves you.* That's the gist of this whole love thing – reaching an ACTIVE state of loving others as God loves us.

Much of the Bible is about *believe and do, hear and go,* and *tell and show.* Like our faith and belief, our love is activated and strengthened by what we hear and see. We follow through on what we have faith for, what we believe in and what we love by *doing* something. My favorite verse to this effect is *Jeremiah 1:12* NKJV:

> Then the LORD said to me, "You have seen well, for I am ready to perform My word."

Are you performing God's word? Are you even receptive to his message? Do you see what He is trying to show you? If you are able to see what He is showing you, are you carrying out His instructions? We're told to love one another. To pray for one another. To submit to one another. To share each other's burdens. To share our possessions so none of us is lacking. We are instructed to have the same mind. Yet somehow, those of us in Christ invariably go wrong.

Use things, not people

> We love each other because He loved us first.
> ~ *1 John 4:19*

One person can love; however love is most effective and powerful when it's reciprocated. In other words, love is most *active* when both parties in a relationship are givers and receivers of love. Similar to our relationship with God – we can't tap into His power and blessings until we receive Him and accept all He offers – we can't truly benefit from our interpersonal relationships until we do the same for the other person in the relationship.

We are able to love because we have first been loved. We are called to go out and love on people so that everyone will experience the love of God. We are to use our gifts and talents in the execution of our commission. We are made to be useful (be of service; serve some purpose) we are not made to be used in a consumptive way (destructive, wasteful).

If you take or receive from someone (love, friendship, tenderness, kindness, housing, transportation, support, you name the resource) without giving anything back, then you're a user. You're consuming and depleting a resource.

When you *give*, you shouldn't expect anything in return. However, when you share (participate in, enjoy, take part jointly, receive equally), there is a definite expectation to receive something in return. When you share yourself with someone, there's an expectation for that person to share themselves with you.

Think of an exchange between yourself and your best friend. You first bonded over a secret or shared experience. Had your friend not reciprocated either with their secrets or experiences, how close do you think you'd be? Probably not very. You're close because you recognized a likeness, a similarity, in each other. That recognition came from sharing something meaningful to each of you.

People who use other people are selfish. They are not looking for shared experiences. They're interested only in opportunities to take advantage of someone to improve their own situation.

However, sharing life experiences will get you much further than using someone for what life has given them.

What have you done for me lately?

> *"Those who accept My commandments and obey them are the ones who love Me. And because they love Me, My Father will love them. And I will love them and reveal Myself to each of them."*
>
> *~ John 14:21*

God said it first: *try me, test me, prove me and see what I will DO for you.* He, in turn, tests us, examines us, and searches us to make us aware of what we are doing for Him.

Love does. It gives and shares. Love is active. It shows up. Love cannot co-habit with fear and it doesn't hide itself.

> *And as we live in God, our love grows more perfect. So we will not be afraid on the day of judgment, but we can face Him with confidence because we live like Jesus here in this world. Such love has no fear, because perfect love expels all fear. If we are afraid, it is for fear of punishment, and this shows that we have not fully experienced His perfect love.*
>
> *~ 1 John 4:17-18*

I take issue with people who try to censor me or hide me away. To me, it expresses a lack of appreciation for who I am. Appreciation is an expression of love (recognition of the quality, value, significance, or magnitude of people and things – an expression of gratitude).

When you start to examine people based on their actions, you see a lot more of how they really feel about you. That's not to say you're comparing yourself to others. You're comparing one person to them self - you're reviewing their action record. For example, if a male friend holds the door open for every female in his radius, but as you (a female friend) approach, he walks through first and allows the door to slam in your face, you would doubt his care and respect for you. Or if a female friend sets a beautiful table and serves an elegant plate to all her guests but when she gets to you (a male friend), she dumps the food on in a pile; you would then doubt her consideration and love for you. These are simple illustrations but they're indicative of people who are not trying to *show* love. They're not trying to give it. They're not trying to share it.

In our flesh, we want to pull away from such people – the ones who react harshly to the gentleness with which we try to live our lives. That's the struggle. Hosea left. He was told to go back. I leave too. I've gotten good at walking away from painful relationships. But I, too, have felt the call to return. I have always gone back to try *one more time* to reach out in kindness and gentleness. To be self-controlled and patient. To offer all of my joy and none of my sadness. That has been how I've shown love to the people in my life.

Love is not a game of Hide 'n Seek

> *Now we see things imperfectly as in a cloudy mirror, but then we will see everything with perfect clarity. All that I know now is partial and incomplete, but then I will know everything completely, just as God now knows me completely.*
>
> *Three things will last forever — faith, hope, and love — and the greatest of these is love.*
>
> *~ 1 Corinthians 13:12-13*

People in the world will mess you up. It took a great deal of time, effort and concentration for me to focus on God's character defining love. I had to let go of and forget the treatment I had received from people who said they loved me but never showed me love. Because of their way of expressing "love," it was hard for me to trust and surrender to God when I first acknowledged my spiritual journey – my life walk with my Lord. I had to purge myself of what I knew from the world, and act in faith according to what I believed in the spirit. Then I had to become open to the full cycle of giving *and* receiving.

Years ago I heard a quote: "Everything is love; hurt and anger only try to mask it." It's not really possible to hide love. That quote got me through a lot of hurt and many stages of anger. I eventually became willing to express myself more fully, which in turn made me more receptive to other people's self-expression. I stopped running from other people's anger, and stayed around to try to resolve the issue. I stopped avoiding hurt and faced it in an attempt to soothe it.

Don't you want to show yourself clearly and be known fully by someone? With no fear of recrimination, rejection or judgment? The best way is to boldly reveal yourself and accept others in their true state as well. When you remove the reason for hiding, fear has no opportunity to root itself in you.

When you channel God's love into your life, most grievances will be covered – set aside, forgiven, forgotten, become a non-issue *(1 Peter 4:8)*. God's love makes it easier to forgive people and continue to build relationships with them. It makes it easier to love and continue to support your loved ones and strangers alike. It's easier for two people to submit (defer to another's judgment, opinion, decision) to one another in various matters. God's love is a unifier and makes it easier for us to share the same mind. How fortunate for us that the love of God does all this and more for us so we can in turn do the same for others – pull them from their dark hiding places (when they're ready) and cover them in love (when we're able). Protect them, nourish them, and build them up. This process is made possible through your openness, through knowing other people and making yourself known to them.

Share yourself and spread the Love

> *This is My commandment: Love each other in the same way I have loved you. There is no greater love than to lay down one's life for one's friends.*
>
> *~ John 15:12-13*

God is selfless in all He has done and continues to do for mankind. His intent is that we would be just as selfless with one another. So get to work! Come out of hiding. Approach boldly and reveal yourself. Put the truth of *action* behind your words. Go, show your love! Prove it! You are made perfect in love, for God is your designer and your example. He loved you first so you can shower others with the love you have for Him. Amen!

I Love You, but God Loves You More

For God loved the world so much that He gave His one and only Son, so that everyone who believes in Him will not perish but have eternal life.
John 3:16

In her book, *Beauty for Ashes*, Joyce Meyer states that her mandate from God is to tell His people He loves them. (Meyer, 1994)

I think about those words often.

Early in my walk, I had a pastor who spent several months teaching on love. I thought I knew what love was until I learned who God is. The pastor told a story about one of the elders in the church who had recently died. The man had run with a rough crew growing up. When he got into the Word and learned about love, he realized the men he'd hung around had never hugged or expressed their love for each other. The elder had told the pastor that one day, as he was ending a call with one of his male friends, he said, "I love you, man." And his friend responded in kind. The elder shared with the pastor that his whole crew was transformed with that simple expression and he was the only one, at that point, living in the Word.

That story plucks chords in me. The power of the Word resonates. It heals. It waters. It grows. It saves. It's life.

> *"God sent His Son into the world not to judge the world, but to save the world through Him."*
>
> *~ John 3:17*

A short time after I heard that story, I spoke to an old friend. At that point we had known each other for ten years. Our relationship began as roommates and continued long after and through long distances. As I ended the call with her that day, I said, "Love ya, girl." She responded, "Don't say that too loud! People aren't going to take it right!"

I was perplexed. "Why would I care how anyone takes it?"

"Do you tell your other friends you love them?"

"Actually, I do." The conversation segued, but I continued to think about her response. I had certainly told her I loved her before. We signed all our cards in love. I traveled to participate in her life events and made sure I acknowledged the annual celebrations. My love and appreciation of her friendship had certainly been expressed. How could she be so uncomfortable with the voicing of it on an ordinary day?

Then it hit me: she was only familiar with the world concept of love. In her limited understanding, love was only for family and spouses. It wasn't something that was shared with friends.

That was a sad realization for me. Through the years, I thought our relationship had grown. But I was the one growing. Though she listened and provided lip service for the lessons I shared with her, she didn't really share my beliefs. She believes there's a God but He's more abstract than active to her. Once in a while, she expressed interest in learning Him for herself and I pointed her to scriptures that seemed to fit what she was looking for. I can only hope the way I live is more encouragement than deterrent for her. The bottom line was we didn't have a shared foundation of faith.

Because of that, the more I grew in the Word of God, the more this friend and I grew apart. I have since learned that God is intent on separating Believers from nonbelievers. If you're fighting such a separation process, please meditate on *2 Corinthians 6:14:*

> *Do not be unequally yoked together with unbelievers. For what fellowship has righteousness with lawlessness? And what communion has light with darkness?*

Separation from nonbelievers does not apply to our individual ministry. We are called to minister to those who don't know Jesus. However, ministering to them – sharing Jesus, God and the Holy Spirit – is different from having a lifestyle that is shared with and influenced by nonbelievers. Hearing this may not be palatable to you, but I would much rather speak and hear objections than to say nothing and have you wonder, because *an open rebuke is better than hidden love (Proverbs 27:5)!* You are responsible for cleaning up your life. When you seek God, He will help you with all manner of cleansings.

Dear Reader – My Brother – My Sister, I love you! And God, our Heavenly Father, wants you to know He loves you so much more. He's the best lover ever! Try Him! In order for you to know and accept that, you must know who He is. God *is* love.

> *God showed how much He loved us by sending His one and only Son into the world so that we might have eternal life through Him. This is real love — not that we loved God, but that He loved us and sent His Son as a sacrifice to take away our sins.*
>
> *Dear friends, since God loved us that much, we surely ought to love each other. No one has ever seen God. But if we love each other, God lives in us, and His love is brought to full expression in us.*

> *We know how much God loves us, and we have put our trust in His love.*
>
> *God is love, and all who live in love live in God, and God lives in them.*
>
> ~ 1 John 4:9-12, 16

Ministry of Reconciliation

There have been many times when I have scolded myself for being a pushover. When others take advantage of me, I get angry with myself more than I do with them. Primarily because those taking advantage have usually learned that I'm a peacemaker at heart and they exploit that character trait in me.

I acknowledge my wrongs when I am aware of them and seek to make amends quickly. When I am hurt, I let the offender know what they did that pained me and then attempt to talk through the issue to a resolution.

In the world, some people may see me as a wimp – a weakling. I've always hated the thought of people perceiving me that way. But getting comfortable in the Word of God has allowed me to let go of the frustration associated with people's erroneous conclusions about me. It's amazing consolation to know that not only am I a peacemaker at heart, but a ministry of reconciliation has been placed in me by my Creator as well. All those years the world showed me no appreciation I was actually functioning within a call I wasn't yet aware of.

> *And all of this is a gift from God, who brought us back to Himself through Christ. And God has given us this task of reconciling people to Him. For God was in Christ, reconciling the world to Himself, no longer counting people's sins against them. And He gave us this wonderful message of reconciliation. So we are Christ's ambassadors; God is making His appeal*

> through us. We speak for Christ when we plead, "Come back to God!" For God made Christ, who never sinned, to be the offering for our sin, so that we could be made right with God through Christ.
> ~ 2 Corinthians 5:18-21

Light of the World

> For God, who said, "Let there be light in the darkness," has made this light shine in our hearts so we could know the glory of God that is seen in the face of Jesus Christ.
> ~ 2 Corinthians 4:6

I work as an executive assistant in my daily life. Administrative assistant work was the only work I could get full-time when I moved to New York City five years ago. I had never before considered it as a career option for me. However I am a very good support person. So good in fact, that even the more difficult managers I have worked with, who complained and belittled me daily, never said a cross word about my work ethic or the quality of my results. Even the worst of my managers complimented me on those traits. Within two years of my arrival in New York City, I began considering making administrative support my career. By my third year, I was able to see how it modeled my work for the Lord.

In the Kingdom of Heaven, I have a Boss who assigned a Personal Trainer to get me ready for my job assignments here on Earth. Everything I do in my assignments is a reflection of my training and my Trainer. In addition to that, I am a representative of my Boss in everything I do here on Earth.

When I received that understanding, I gained a greater appreciation for my nine-to-five assignment. I appreciated being placed in a position to assist someone daily. It's a servant position that keeps me servant-minded. Being servant-minded keeps me humble and open to assisting many others in whatever capacity I am able to do so.

As Christ's ambassador, I am His assistant. I am functioning in the flesh in His stead. That is a very important correlation to make.

My first year-end performance review for my current position took place six months after I started. My manager, who I call Boss Lady, (she prefers Bossy) will most likely go down in my work history as the best boss ever (on Earth). But for now I'll be modest and say she's second only to the manager who trained me into restaurant management nearly fifteen years ago. That was another servant-minded work environment with an emphasis on hospitality. I learned lessons there that I still apply to life and work.

In my performance review, Boss Lady said, "You have such a wonderful attitude, you make coming to work enjoyable for me. And people enjoy dealing with you. I like that, because you're my ambassador. You're my representative to people who are trying to reach me. I appreciate knowing they're in good hands with you."

Think about that...

Honestly, even as she said those words, I felt as if God were speaking to me. She used Kingdom words and I heard Him telling me I was doing a good job in the situations He placed me in.

You're my representative to people who are trying to reach me.

That's what we are called to do by the Boss of bosses! In 2 Corinthians 5:20, we learn we are Christ's ambassadors, through whom God makes His appeal to the world. If God were to give you a performance review today, what do you think He'd say? I'm certain He'd want to know: *Do His people know He loves them? Did you go and continue forth as sent? Is your light shining in the darkness? Do you walk around with the face of Jesus Christ? Have you walked a distance with the people you helped to salvation? Or did you just leave them at the door?*

We have to follow-through on our assignments. For example, an older lady at church once told me how she gave advice to a young lady who was experiencing difficulties in her life. The young woman wanted someone to confide in and had expressed her need for spiritual guidance. The elder lady replied by giving the young lady her email and church addresses. That's all. That was the elder's only reply to a woman standing in front of her expressing her need for assistance and love – a woman who was actively seeking the way and verbalizing her request for help.

The young lady said, "But... how do I speak to you?"

The elder replied, "Email me or find me at church."

Our job is not done by just handing out information or providing a general direction in which information might be found. We are to be helpers – assistants to our fellows here on Earth. The elder lady's response sounded cold and disconnected when she shared the story with me. Quite honestly, I'd be surprised to learn the young lady had ever come to the church at all. That was a God-opportunity for the elder to be the face of Christ. We can repeat *John 3:16* but it converts best when we live it.

You are the Son. You're the *One* God gave to the world. You need to represent the Kingdom to the best of the ability God put in you. As great as a church building or services may be, the building or services aren't sent to bring people to Christ, we are *(Matthew 10:5-8)*. We are the attraction that lures people of the world towards the light of Heaven. The building isn't the temple of God, our bodies are *(1 Corinthians 6:19)*. Do your job, be a living sacrifice *(Romans 12:1-2)*. Give your time. Give your love. Give of yourself. Let God's glory shine through you *(1 Corinthians 10:31-33)*. Know that you are loved and you are Love's ambassador. Tell His people, their Father God loves them.

Are You Ready For Love?

This is my commandment: Love each other in the same way I have loved you. There is no greater love than to lay down one's life for one's friends.
John 15:13-14

We ask many questions in our relationships in a quest to get to know the other person. In return, we share a good deal of personal information about ourselves in an attempt to be known.

In my book, *My God and Me: Listening, Learning and Growing on My Journey,* I entreated everyone in my life, all my readers and anyone yet to cross my path, to allow me to love them. The piece is titled, *Can I Love You?* (Jones, 2009) *Can I Love You* was written within two years of consciously beginning my walk with God. It was a question I wanted to ask all the people who seemed to be pushing me away and shutting me out.

That piece came about when I realized I had been on a love-quest, in search of people to love. That search was the most difficult and labor-intensive activity I've ever attempted. Why? Because I was trying to love everyone. The pain came when I realized everyone doesn't know how to be loved. (Jones, 2009) Even if they were interested in receiving love, they weren't ready for it.

Can I love you? became a meditative question for over two years. I was trying to understand the people I had opened my heart and life to, who, in return, slammed their doors in my face and turned their backs on me.

The question I asked was a very passive and humbling approach to express a willingness and availability to love openly without reservations. What I came to understand during the writing of that piece is that people who fear rejection are most likely to reject others first so they can avoid being rejected themselves.

That's good information to have. It has brought me to my current meditative question: *are you ready for love?* It's a more direct question. It removes the focus from me and puts emphasis on you. It's no longer about what I have to give; now it's about what you're able to receive.

Are you ready to give love?

> *There is no greater love than to lay down one's life for one's friends.*
>
> *~ John 15:13*

Jesus said that there is no greater love than to sacrifice your own life for your friends. He fulfilled His calling to do just that, so we could see that His words are not empty rhetoric.

What are you ready to do to show love to your friends, to your family, to your spouse? What are you sacrificing in your life for them? What are you giving of yourself to your relationships?

Ephesians 5:28-29 gives another excellent illustration on how to give and show love:

> *In the same way, husbands ought to love their wives as they love their own bodies. For a man who loves his wife actually shows love for himself. No one hates his*

own body but feeds and cares for it, just as Christ cares for the church.

It's only difficult to love another as you love yourself if you are not in right standing in your relationship with God. If you don't have a relationship with God, the thing you know as love will more than likely be something destructive to human life. If a relationship is not caring and nurturing, love is not present. The act of loving someone is an expression of love for yourself and for the Christ in you. When you are able to acknowledge that and project it, you are ready to give love. All other objections are simple sleight-of-hand illusions.

Are you ready to receive love?
Perhaps it's easier to give than to receive, but both are equally important. Relationships are successful and prosper because of the flow and cycle of giving and receiving – as an exchange of equals. The process of giving and receiving oils the wheels of any relationship. When one aspect is absent from either party, the relationship gets rocky and uncertain.

Nothing in the Kingdom of Heaven is forced on you. God doesn't force His love or His presence on anyone. No one is forced to believe in Him, His Son, His Holy Spirit or any of the written words in the Bible. We all have a choice to do so. He wants us to choose Him – thereby choosing life and love. He hopes for us to believe on His Son, Jesus Christ, and to accept His Holy Spirit in the temple of our bodies. But He is not going to make us do so.

We have to make a decision, a conscious choice, to accept what is on offer.

> *"Today I have given you the choice between life and death, between blessings and curses. Now I call on*

> *Heaven and Earth to witness the choice you make. Oh, that you would choose life, so that you and your descendants might live! You can make this choice by loving the LORD your God, obeying Him, and committing yourself firmly to Him. This is the key to your life."*
>
> *~ Deuteronomy 30:19-20*

The whole of God's Word is based on a choice between life and death. He says clearly in *Deuteronomy 30:19* that He wants us to choose life. Evidence of our choosing life is how we show love to God. It is impossible to love God if we have not first accepted and received His words and love. By choosing life, there is a conscious choice to receive love.

If you are unable to receive love, you have not fully received God into your heart and life. You're holding something back. You're hiding. You're hanging onto fear and misconceptions. I can say this because I know what love is *(1 Corinthians 13:4-8).* Love *does not* coexist with fear in any form.

> *Such love has no fear, because perfect love expels all fear. If we are afraid, it is for fear of punishment, and this shows that we have not fully experienced His perfect love. We love each other because He loved us first.*
>
> *~ 1 John 4:18-19*

In order to accept God fully, you must first surrender to Him completely. When we allow our sinful nature to die in Christ, we are then granted life with Him eternally. We can't keep some of our sin and expect any part of eternity. A half-hearted, lukewarm Christian is despised by Him *(Revelation 3:16).* So, make up your mind and seek Him with all your passion – heart, soul, mind and strength.

> *But I am trusting you, O LORD, saying, "You are my God!" My future is in your hands.*
> ~ *Psalm 31:14-15*

Can you say that? Can you speak it and believe it? If so, do it. Tell God that you yield control of your life to Him. By yielding control of your life, you are accepting delivery of His love. (That's the most awesome exchange I've ever made!)

When you have accepted and received God fully, accepting and receiving love from your interpersonal relationships will be much easier. You'll already have a personal model to go by, as our relationship with the Lord is a guidepost for all our other relationships.

Perhaps you still have some hurdles you have to get over and becoming ready to receive love doesn't appear as simple as "accept God and love from others will flow into you." But it is that simple. God is all. He's the beginning and the end. Our struggle in relationships has more to do with our struggle with Him than with the other person. If you're excellent at giving and receiving love, repentance and forgiveness and your relationships are still difficult, then perhaps it's the other people's relationship with God that is the issue. Tongue in cheek, but not completely! There is a need to build relationships on the foundation of God's Word – at least your intimate relationships with spouses, parents, and friends.

First Fruits of All Your Crops

Honor the LORD with your wealth and with the best part of everything you produce. Then he will fill your barns with grain, and your vats will overflow with good wine.
Proverbs 3:9-10

I am not a financial tither and I believe what most churches teach about financial tithing is unscriptural. However, I do give financial gifts to my church and other charitable organizations. More importantly, I give generously of myself and my possessions – knowing that I am only a steward who truly owns nothing.

Tithing Truths

According to some of the rhetoric taught in churches today, I should be damned with a curse *(Malachi 3:10)* because they say that the *only* way to *really* worship God is with money. That has never made sense to me. And the more I study, the more outrageous a lie it appears to be.

> *wealth*
> 1. *a great quantity or store of money, valuable possessions, property, or other riches*
> 2. *an abundance or profusion of anything; plentiful amount*
> 3. *rich or valuable contents or produce*
> 4. *the state of being rich; prosperity; affluence*
> *(Dictionary.com, 2010)*

The scriptures on which I base my viewpoint are listed below. Ironically, I'll begin with *Malachi 3:8-11:*

> *"Should people cheat God? Yet you have cheated Me!*
>
> *"But you ask, 'What do you mean? When did we ever cheat You?'*
>
> *"You have cheated Me of the tithes and offerings due to Me. You are under a curse, for your whole nation has been cheating Me. Bring all the tithes into the storehouse so there will be enough food in My Temple. If you do," says the* LORD *of Heaven's Armies, "I will open the windows of Heaven for you. I will pour out a blessing so great you won't have enough room to take it in! Try it! Put Me to the test! Your crops will be abundant, for I will guard them from insects and disease. Your grapes will not fall from the vine before they are ripe," says the* LORD *of Heaven's Armies.*

Malachi 3:10 is usually quoted to support a monetary tithe. However, *Malachi 3:10* reads to me as a promise of a blessing God was sending His people in the form of His Holy Spirit. The New Living Translation version comes across sharper to me than the traditional King James or popular New International versions where "house" is used instead of "temple." This is significant because the New Testament clearly identifies the physical body of the Believer in Christ as a temple of God's Holy Spirit *(1 Corinthians 6:19).* The word of God is described as meat and bread. Food that gives us life *(Matthew 4:4).* And Jesus is the first fruit of God's chosen people *(1 Corinthians 15:20).* None of that is about money. It's about resources that build up God's Kingdom.

In *Acts 2:1-4*, we learn He fulfilled His promise:

> *On the day of Pentecost all the believers were meeting together in one place. Suddenly, there was a sound from*

Heaven like the roaring of a mighty windstorm, and it filled the house where they were sitting. Then, what looked like flames or tongues of fire appeared and settled on each of them. And everyone present was filled with the Holy Spirit and began speaking in other languages, as the Holy Spirit gave them this ability.

And *Romans 5:5* tells us:

And this hope will not lead to disappointment. For we know how dearly God loves us, because He has given us the Holy Spirit to fill our hearts with His love.

But more importantly, I enjoy listening to Jesus. He was asked a question regarding government taxes, yet replied with an answer on how to *give* to God.

"Should we pay or shouldn't we?"

But Jesus knew their hypocrisy. "Why are you trying to trap Me?" He asked. "Bring Me a denarius and let Me look at it." They brought the coin, and He asked them, "Whose portrait is this? And whose inscription?"

"Caesar's," they replied.

Then Jesus said to them, "Give to Caesar what is Caesar's and to God what is God's."

~ *Mark 12:15-17*

Whose face and inscription is on your dollar bill? More directly, what belongs to God? Answer: everything in Heaven and on the Earth *(Psalm 24:1)*. Even more precisely, *people* belong to God. Jesus spoke clearly in *John 4:23-24* when he described exactly what God requires from His worshipers:

Yet a time is coming and has now come when the true worshipers will worship the Father in spirit and truth,

> *for they are the kind of worshipers the Father seeks. God is spirit, and His worshipers must worship in spirit and in truth."*

In spirit and truth — that's the only way to truly worship God. To get this fully, you have to have an understanding of:
1) Shadow effect – the Old Testament hints at the substance in the New Testament by providing physical illustrations and examples of spiritual principles
2) Alternate reality – life in the spirit is true life; the New Testament is the revelation millennia of generations were waiting for
3) Spiritual fruit is good for physical life – you need to appreciate and be open to the fruit of the spirit in order for it to produce in your life

> *But the Holy Spirit produces this kind of fruit in our lives: love, joy, peace, patience, kindness, goodness, faithfulness, gentleness, and self-control. There is no law against these things!*
>
> *~ Galatians 5:22-23*

As long as I walk in God's Word and obey His commands, there is no law against me. I tell you truthfully, my life has prospered with love, joy, peace, patience, kindness, goodness, faithfulness, gentleness and self-control. The more I practice each portion of the fruit of the spirit, the more I increase in this life and in my spirit life.

How do I practice? I practice by loving God first and honoring Him by loving His people. I give of myself, my resources, my gifts and my talents. I do what I can for others when asked and when I simply see a need. The more I increase spiritually, the more I am able to plant spiritual fruit into other peoples' lives. My pet name for this act is *spiritual tithing*, but the simple scriptural word is *give* (to present voluntarily and without expecting compensation). That's what I believe we are intended to do in order to benefit the Kingdom of God.

Money does not benefit God's Kingdom. Money is man-made; it is not a medium of worship. Every man-made or human-centered offering presented to God in the Bible was scorned by Him. Nothing we have is good enough to give to God. Nothing we create is acceptable to Him. God provides His own sacrifice; he tells us what He will accept as an offering. I'll go out on a limb here and say the only thing good enough to offer to God is something He has made for Himself to receive.

At this point in time, what would that be?

Answer: People.

We are not man-made. We were created for a purpose, and one of our design functions is to receive love. We were created to receive God's love and give love back to Him. His original plan was to spend eternity in fellowship with us. His back-up plan allows Believers to spend every day in fellowship with God, because of His indwelling spirit.

In *Romans 12:1*, we are told to give our bodies as a living sacrifice as an act of worship to God.

Please note: the message is not that you should not support your church organization – that is a personal choice you alone make. Again, giving is scriptural. I do give financial gifts to my church organization; I just don't consider them tithes. I consider the gifts to be financial support for organizational needs – maintenance, utilities, services to the community, etc. The message I am attempting to convey is: *monetary tithing* does not progress you in the Kingdom

> *indwell*
> Be permanently present in (someone's soul or mind); possess spiritually
> (Dictionary.com, 2010)

nor does it benefit the Kingdom itself. Ask yourself, "How will the Kingdom of God benefit from my money?" Keep in mind that the Kingdom of God is God's spiritual kingdom, not your physical church community.

On the other hand, the Kingdom of God is benefitted when you share spiritual fruit with others. When you love others, share your joy, spread peace, are patient, kind and good, the people on the receiving end usually can't help but to reciprocate in some way. Such behavior starts a chain of sorts. Sooner or later, someone is going to ask you about your faith, your beliefs, the God you serve and the church you attend. At that point, you know you may have won a soul for Christ, however the work was done long before you spoke a word; you simply watered and nurtured what was in them. That's how we benefit the Kingdom – by giving back to God from the fruit with which He has increased our lives.

Ultimately, however, whether you agree or not, as long as you act according to your beliefs and understanding and do what you do as if you're doing for God (while adhering to His instructions), you remain in right standing with the LORD *(Romans 14:1-8)*. I'm not here to judge your practices; I'm here to share what I've learned from practicing the Word.

> *So Christ has truly set us free. Now make sure that you stay free, and don't get tied up again in slavery to the law.*
>
> *~ Galatians 5:1*

First Fruit

God's greatest blessing to us is not money, a house, a car, a job, a spouse or children. God's greatest gift to his children is the gift of Jesus Christ. You know the verse: *He so LOVED us that He GAVE His only Son (John 3:16)*. God gave of Himself. He continues to give the best of Himself in the form of His Holy Spirit. Nothing else is good enough for Him to receive. By His Spirit we can become holy enough to be received by Him. He is ever ready to receive us to Himself – under His preset conditions. We just have to be willing to turn to Him and do what He requires of us.

> *But in fact, Christ has been raised from the dead. He is the first of a great harvest of all who have died.*
>
> *~1 Corinthians 15:20*

Believers are God's crop and Jesus is His first fruit – His tithe. How are you furthering the Kingdom? What's your crop? What are you producing, growing and gathering? What is your life yielding?

What are you harvesting?

I love the New Living Translation version of the Sower Parable in *Luke 8:5-8*. Jesus Christ is speaking:

Crop, harvest, yield all refer to the return in food obtained from land at the end of a season of growth.

Crop denotes the amount produced at one cutting or for one particular season.

Harvest denotes either the time of reaping and gathering, or the gathering, or that which is gathered.

Yield emphasizes what is given by the land in return for expenditure of time and labor.

(Dictionary.com, 2010)

> "A farmer went out to plant his seed. As he scattered it across his field, some seed fell on a footpath, where it was stepped on, and the birds ate it. Other seed fell among rocks. It began to grow, but the plant soon wilted and died for lack of moisture. Other seed fell among thorns that grew up with it and choked out the tender plants. Still other seed fell on fertile soil. This seed grew and produced a crop that was a hundred times as much as had been planted!"

> *When he had said this, he called out, "Anyone with ears to hear should listen and understand."*

The Disciples asked Jesus what He meant and He told them they were permitted to understand the secrets of the Kingdom of God. Believers need to be told this because the world speaks of God's ways as a mystery. His ways are only a mystery to those in the world. Once you accept His spirit, you have access to understanding His ways. Jesus explained the above parable as follows:

> *"This is the meaning of the parable: The seed is God's word. The seeds that fell on the footpath represent those who hear the message, only to have the devil come and take it away from their hearts and prevent them from believing and being saved. The seeds on the rocky soil represent those who hear the message and receive it with joy. But since they don't have deep roots, they believe for a while, then they fall away when they face temptation. The seeds that fell among the thorns represent those who hear the message, but all too quickly the message is crowded out by the cares and riches and pleasures of this life. And so they never grow into maturity. And the seeds that fell on the good soil represent honest, good-hearted people who hear God's word, cling to it, and patiently produce a huge harvest.*
> *~ Luke 8:11-15*

I accept my commission. I am good, fertile soil that is patiently producing a huge harvest for God. In order for God's seed in me to increase, I must multiply what He planted in me. Therefore I too become a farmer, planting seed (God's Word) into others (for example, you and others who encounter my writings). I'm tithing myself. I'm giving the best of my spirit to other people. In doing so, I'm giving back to God what belongs to Him.

What's your crop? After your season of growth, how are you getting your harvest to market? This is a beautiful visual! I know many people who overcame major struggles yet they never speak of their journey, their lesson or their growth. In fact, they don't view the struggles as anything spiritual at all. And they repeat the same mistakes throughout their life. Then there are people who learn well from their struggles but they never share their lessons either. They keep their growth to themselves as their own personal business not to be shared with anyone who doesn't need to know about it.

Neither group is marketing their harvest – their testimony of what God has done in their life. That portion of their life becomes something of a wasted season.

I market my harvest through my writing. I write about my growth and experiences in the Word. In the midst of each growing season I take stock of where I was before, and take notes on the process until it's completed. At the end of the growing season, I gather everything I learned and experienced for reflection. In this way I am better prepared for the seasons to come.

When I gave my talent over completely to the service of God's Kingdom – writing about how He's moving in me - my life increased and prospered in ways I can't adequately convey to you. Please don't mistake that as a claim to financial wealth. Though I'm comfortably past struggling to pay for my financial needs, every paycheck I receive counts!

What I mean is, every time I learn something in this process of life, I share it. I don't keep it to myself, hide it or bury it *(Matthew 25:24)*. I shine a light on it and offer it as a seed to plant into someone else's life. The most significant offering I can make to

God's Kingdom is giving of myself openly, fully, and honestly. In so doing, I am sharing the Christ in me – the best of all offerings.

> *And I am praying that you will put into action the generosity that comes from your faith as you understand and experience all the good things we have in Christ. Your love has given me much joy and comfort, my brother, for your kindness has often refreshed the hearts of God's people.*
>
> *~ Philemon 1:6-7*

May God bless and prosper you in His ways.

What Makes You Happy?

Above all, love each other deeply, because love covers over a multitude of sins.
1 Peter 4:8

I had a friend who watched her favorite romantic drama, *The Notebook,* two weeks before her wedding to a man she had been with for a number of years.

As she sat on her sofa crying, she lamented that her love didn't seem to hold a candle to the love chronicled in that movie. When her fiancé came home that night, she was in tears and he, a pragmatic man, asked what was wrong and what could he do to help. She replied, "Give me *The Notebook* type of love!"

"What's the notebook," he asked.

To my friend, this sounded like irrefutable confirmation that he was most certainly not the one for her. But being a generous woman, she gave him the DVD and asked him to watch it and get back to her.

I don't know if he ever watched the movie and, if he did, if he got anything from it. But I do know I had to shake my friend awake! *Gurl! Don't you let yo' man go because of The Notebook!* That was a good conversation....

She had gotten sidetracked by the fiery sparks, electric passion and timeless way love is depicted by a huge budget and a great storyteller in a soft-lit Hollywood romance. She wanted to be swept up in the rain in a wild, reckless passion. She wanted her eyes to light up when she spoke of him. She wanted to feel tingles whenever she thought of him. Unfortunately, she was feeling trapped in the mechanics of life and couldn't grasp that love was actually carrying her through it all.

She has since thanked me repeatedly for what I said that day. I don't remember all the words I had for her, but I recall the general message: "I don't know your fiancé; I only know what you've told me about him. According to you, he's a good man. I can only take you at your word. At no point have you said you no longer love him. You think you're missing out on one element in your relationship – romance. I'm gonna tell ya, no one has it all." Then I listed all the things he had done for her and her daughter over the years, from her own words. All the ways he had proven himself her loyal supporter, faithful provider, constant friend, adamant advocate and yes, even her beloved lover. He not only impressed her with his unfailingly active presence in her life, he impressed people listening in on their life (i.e. me).

Many people have romance, however, not as many have a relationship in which you can see God actively living. I saw that with them.

Going through the rockiness of the final month leading up to their wedding didn't prepare me for the awesome glow emanating from them both during their ceremony. I was mesmerized. Especially when they danced their first dance as man and wife to "Go Light Your World" by Kathy Troccoli. My friend thought her love paled in comparison to *The Notebook*, I told her on her wedding day, "The way he looks at you is better than anything in *The Notebook!*"

Have you thought about what you *think* would make you happy versus what *actually* makes you happy? After years in her relationship, when it came down to the wire, my friend feared she might be settling. We can call it cold feet or second thoughts, whichever – she was contemplating trading in the real thing to go search for an illusion.

I know she is extremely happy with her decision and her commitment, and I am extremely happy for her. They have my heartfelt prayers and congratulations for their union.

I've thought about what truly makes me happy. Love does it for me. Seeing *love* in action, feeling *love* move, giving *love* my attention, experiencing *love* in daily life, being surrounded by *love* in others and witnessing *love* perform miracles. Pretty much any manifestation of LOVE makes me happy.

I love experiencing love all around me. I look forward to a life in which I am in constant receipt of love from family and friends. Until that time, my purest joy comes from giving love to others by sharing myself fully in whatever way I can.

Power of Love

For in Him we live and move and exist.
Acts 17:28

How powerful is love?
Apart from it, we are nothing.
Love transforms. It heals. It builds. It covers. Protects. Nurtures. Helps. Gives. Forgives. Receives. Opens hearts. Offers security. Love restores and breathes life into people and relationships.

Love is powerful. It's a word many people want to hear in their lives. When applied to action, it changes lives. When acknowledged as the essence of God, life will never be the same.

Song of Solomon 8:6 says:

> *For love is as strong as death, its jealousy as enduring as the grave.*

The translation that pierced my heart is from Meister Eckhart von Hochheim: *Love is as strong as death, as hard as hell. Death separates the soul from the body, but love separates all things from the soul.*

Meditate on that for a moment.

> *Can anything ever separate us from Christ's love? No, despite all these things, overwhelming victory is ours through Christ, who loved us. And I am convinced that*

nothing can ever separate us from God's love. Neither death nor life, neither angels nor demons, neither our fears for today nor our worries about tomorrow — not even the powers of hell can separate us from God's love. No power in the sky above or in the Earth below — indeed, nothing in all creation will ever be able to separate us from the love of God that is revealed in Christ Jesus our Lord.

~ Romans 8:35, 37-39

Life and death are spoken of both in physical and spiritual terms in the Bible. Physical life and death are temporary. We are exhorted to concern ourselves with spiritual life and avoid spiritual death, both of which are eternal. A spiritual life involves unity with God and spiritual death is complete separation from God.

True love, God's love, will clean up your life. When you surrender everything you are and all you have, He will take control of you and direct yours steps. His Holy Spirit will cleanse and purify you. God erects a wall around His chosen people and ejects those who would taint His relationship with His chosen ones. After a while, the Believer's conviction becomes their filter for the world. They become able to identify those people and situations that don't resemble their God and willingly turn away from them. When you trust the Lord your God, He will separate you from everything in the world that is not like Him. He is benevolent and compassionate, but also jealous and territorial. He wants His people to remain His. No worries, once you are counted among His children you will want to stay in the family as well!

When Your Love is Rejected

> Then Jesus told them, "A prophet is honored everywhere except in his own hometown and among his own family." And so He did only a few miracles there because of their unbelief.
> Matthew 13:57-58

Love is the most rejected resource on Earth.

When you practice loving others, you quickly realize people aren't so interested in what you have to offer. You also learn that love is not something you can force on others. Just like it's a choice to love, it is also a choice to receive love. It's akin to a game of catch (though I detest the thought of love being a game). A game of catch is only engaged when the tossed ball is accepted and returned. When one person puts the ball down and walks away from it, the game ends. Of course, loving people isn't so simple, but the analogy is a better illustration of love as a fluid action of giving and receiving.

When relationships are over

Some time ago, the phrase "it is finished" looped on replay in my mind in the context of the dead relationships in my life. For the last several years, I had been trying to maintain, revitalize, pump up and get things started in various relationships. It took me a while to realize that God was separating me from not only the nonbelievers in my life, but also from the relationships that weren't bearing good fruit. Once that realization came, it was easy to let go of people who didn't want to be held.

> *So every tree that does not produce good fruit is chopped down and thrown into the fire. Yes, just as you can identify a tree by its fruit, so you can identify people by their actions.*
>
> *~ Matthew 7:19-20*

Late last spring, I had a dream that would have been disturbing, if taken at face value, but it proved to be a reassuring message instead.

I don't recall the sequence but there was a scene in which all types of bugs were seen crawling around a sleeping body when a light was flipped on. There was a scene of a big, dark, empty room penetrated by several beams of light coming through a torn and drooping curtain. Then the most potentially disturbing scene was that of a decomposing body lying in the corner with the head stuck to a mop. Sounds gritty and nasty, I know. You're probably wondering where the relief came in. After each scene the room was flooded by a bucket of hot, soapy water. The bugs were washed away, the curtain was fixed and pushed back to let more light in and the decomposing body was removed and the area it infected was cleaned. The scenes went on in a rotation with each one slightly different than the one before. The little bugs were washed away, but later one huge, animal-size flying bug unfolded on a counter top. The decomposing body was removed with the mop, but then the mop was needed to clean the floor, so the body had to be approached and disconnected from the mop in order to better clean the floor. Again, each scene ended with a full cleaning of the room and exposure to additional light.

I awoke feeling as if some work had been completed.

Whatever I had been doing that was not bearing fruit, I felt free to withdraw from. Whatever was weighing me down and blocking my light was being removed from my life. My Father was cleansing me. He was washing away all the darkness and ushering me further into His Light.

God requires obedience, faithfulness, respect, loyalty and a continued hope in Him. In return we receive His love, mercy, grace and salvation – actually that's all on offer before we are placed in the womb. But we have to *accept it all* in order to *benefit* from it all. Our obedience is proof of our love of Him – keeping his law, adhering to his commands. Though His nature is love and He gives love unconditionally, we have the option to reject His love. Astounding, really – rejecting love; turning your back and walking away from it. But we have the choice to do that; the "freedom" to do as we please. However, the consequence of our choosing against God, life and love is that He then chooses not to fellowship with us. Our choices either unite us with God or separate us from Him. He tells us to make ourselves holy for Him because He is holy. He wants fellowship, but there are requirements we have to meet.

> *For I am the LORD your God. You shall therefore consecrate yourselves, and you shall be holy; for I am holy.*
>
> ~ *Leviticus 11:44*

Follow me here: If we model our relationships after the prototype God has given us for our relationship with Him, there are basic things that both parties have to contribute to any relationship (be it friend, family, spouse, employment, etc.) for it to be successful. There needs to be an obedience/adherence to and respect for the foundation and expectation laid for the relationship (i.e. boundaries). There needs to be loyalty, faithfulness and a hope for continued growth and improvement. There needs to be a consciousness of and an effort to meet the requirements of the other party in the relationship. When both parties are giving and doing all that (and more, according to the needs of the individuals), then each party will bask in the other's grace, mercy and covering.

> *And above all things have fervent love for one another, for "love will cover a multitude of sins."*
> ~ *1 Peter 4:8 NKJ*

However, when love, loyalty, faithfulness, and respect are lacking from either party to the other, the relationship becomes stagnant, it becomes a dead weight – a decomposing corpse. Relationships aren't intended to be one-sided. Yes, God loves you unconditionally, but even He has requirements of you in order for you to reap the benefits of His love.

For those of you not doing your portion of the work in your relationships, wake up before you're washed away. And for those of you toiling alone, think about breaking ground elsewhere. When the other party in the relationship you're toiling in doesn't accept or receive you, and you've done everything you know to do, it's okay to let go and move on. That has been a hard lesson to learn, but I finally got it – not every situation I contribute to (sow into) will grow the expected or hoped-for fruit. Sometimes the fruit grown from a seed I plant may not be for me to harvest. It may not even be for me to water it. It may just be for me to plant the seed and move on. We will reap what we sow, but there's no promise to reap *where* we sow.

> *Therefore, brothers, since we have confidence to enter the Most Holy Place by the blood of Jesus, by a new and living way opened for us through the curtain, that*

is, his body, and since we have a great priest over the house of God, let us draw near to God with a sincere heart in full assurance of faith, having our hearts sprinkled to cleanse us from a guilty conscience and having our bodies washed with pure water.

~ Hebrews 10:19-22

Repentance

Prove by the way you live that you have repented of your sins and turned to God.
Luke 3:8

What does it mean to "repent"?

You showed that you have done everything necessary to make things right.
2 Corinthians 7:11

Repent is a word not often spoken in contemporary culture. We as individuals are told to be ourselves, do what we want, live as we please and enjoy life. But, invariably, following one or all of these cultural myths will lead to someone in our life getting hurt by something we say or do. As a result, our relationships suffer. Though suffering is a part of life and we grow most through our struggles, the unfortunate truth is that most people try to avoid suffering and speed through their struggles – getting as little as possible from the experiences.

The self-centered person will not take the time to focus on the individual they hurt. And the hurt individual will, sometimes, try to hide their pain, or simply "get over it" on their own. Neither of these approaches improves nor strengthens the relationship.

In our contemporary language we "apologize" or say we're "sorry" for causing offense. However, neither being sorry (feeling regret, sorrow, grief or sadness) or offering an apology (expressing regret, remorse or sorrow for having insulted, failed, injured, or wronged another) is the same as repenting (to feel such sorrow for sin or fault as to be disposed to change one's life for the better).

I had a male acquaintance who used to apologize for not following through on his word. Every time he disappointed me, he admitted his failure. After so many apologies, I asked him why he bothered to say anything at all if he continued to behave the same manner. His response: he continued his hurtful behavior but omitted his apologies.

He completely missed the point. And I blamed myself for not expressing my frustration in a clearer manner. In addition to that, my desire to be a loving Christian led me to repeatedly pardon his dismissive behavior. In effect, I enabled him to continue treating me in a way that hurt and belittled me. It was obvious I valued the relationship and equally obvious how little value he placed on it and me.

He did not change his behavior, therefore he did not repent. Eventually, I reached a point where I could no longer ignore my pain and I sought to disassociate myself from him completely.

As our relationship with God exhibits, all relationships are salvageable. There simply has to be a desire within both parties to do what is necessary to restore the relationship. In the case of my former acquaintance, he would have to give me what I desire – true repentance.

> Now I am glad I sent it [letter], not because it hurt you, but because the pain caused you to repent and change your ways. It was the kind of sorrow God wants His people to have, so you were not harmed by us in any way. For the kind of sorrow God wants us to experience leads us away from sin and results in salvation. There's no regret for that kind of sorrow. But worldly sorrow, which lacks repentance, results in spiritual death.
>
> Just see what this godly sorrow produced in you! Such earnestness, such concern to clear yourselves, such

> *indignation, such alarm, such longing to see me, such zeal, and such a readiness to punish wrong. You showed that you have done everything necessary to make things right. My purpose, then, was not to write about who did the wrong or who was wronged. I wrote to you so that in the sight of God you could see for yourselves how loyal you are to us.*
> ~ *2 Corinthians 7:9-12*

Restoration of our relationship would have to involve the process outlined above. I would have to know that the pain of our broken relationship caused him to change his behavior towards me *(v. 9)*. I would need to see that his desire to reconcile moved him to take action to save the relationship. I would need to know that he does not want our relationship to be one of the dead things in his life *(v.10)*. I would need to experience his earnestness and his true concern for me. I would need to see that there is some alarm at the prospect of our bond being dissolved. He would need to show me that he is doing everything in his power to make amends and that he is indeed loyal to me *(v. 11,12)*.

A flippant "sorry" or "oh, well, I'll do better next time" doesn't even begin to cover all that. When you hold people accountable for their actions against you, you assist them in becoming better citizens of Heaven. You improve their walk as well as your own. In doing so, you both become better representatives of Christ and the God who sent Him.

In each of our human relationships, we are equal parts teacher, student and negotiator. We continuously teach the other person about who we are – our likes, dislikes, boundaries, and goals – while learning the same about them. When disagreements occur, if there's a desire to maintain the relationship, both parties will negotiate for an equally satisfying solution.

Psalm 51

For the choir director: A psalm of David, regarding the time Nathan the prophet came to him after David had committed adultery with Bathsheba.

Have mercy on me, O God, because of Your unfailing love. Because of Your great compassion, blot out the stain of my sins. Wash me clean from my guilt. Purify me from my sin. For I recognize my rebellion; it haunts me day and night. Against You, and You alone, have I sinned; I have done what is evil in Your sight. You will be proved right in what You say, and Your judgment against me is just. For I was born a sinner — yes, from the moment my mother conceived me. But You desire honesty from the womb, teaching me wisdom even there.

Purify me from my sins, and I will be clean; wash me, and I will be whiter than snow. Oh, give me back my joy again; You have broken me — now let me rejoice. Don't keep looking at my sins. Remove the stain of my guilt. Create in me a clean heart, O God. Renew a loyal spirit within me. Do not banish me from Your presence, and don't take Your Holy Spirit from me.

Restore to me the joy of Your salvation, and make me willing to obey You. Then I will teach Your ways to rebels, and they will return to You. Forgive me for shedding blood, O God who saves; then I will joyfully sing of Your forgiveness. Unseal my lips, O Lord, that my mouth may praise You.

You do not desire a sacrifice, or I would offer one. You do not want a burnt offering. The sacrifice You desire is a broken spirit.

You will not reject a broken and repentant heart, O God. Look with favor on Zion and help her; rebuild the walls of Jerusalem. Then You will be pleased with sacrifices offered in the right spirit — with burnt offerings and whole burnt offerings. Then bulls will again be sacrificed on Your altar.

The Psalm 51 Example: Repent and Live

If we claim we have no sin, we are only fooling ourselves and not living in the truth. But if we confess our sins to Him, He is faithful and just to forgive us our sins and to cleanse us from all wickedness. If we claim we have not sinned, we are calling God a liar and showing that His word has no place in our hearts.
1 John 1:8-10

According to the Bible, *repentance* is the ultimate communication leading to forgiveness and resulting in a restored relationship. Repentance consists of:

1. acknowledging your sin (wrongdoing, transgression, offense)
2. accepting responsibility without defending or excusing yourself or your actions
3. understanding the severity and repercussions for what you have done and how it affects your relationship
4. humbling yourself and requesting forgiveness from the one you harmed
5. knowing that mercy and grace are not deserved
6. expressing a sincere desire and intention to change your ways
7. doing what you need to do (i.e. what's requested by or negotiated with the offended person) to restore the relationship.

Psalm 51 is an excellent example of David's true repentance for a very specific sin against God. It's an amazing declaration of his love and devotion to God, as well as an expression of his desire to be cleansed and live as a righteous man. It's an example of how we should seek to heal and restore our relationship with God first, then others.

Repentance is so much more than an apology. It's completely turning away from the course you are on and committing yourself to God's ways. In human relational language: repenting is committing yourself fully to the relationship you are seeking to restore, while staying in alignment with God's laws. Repentance is not something that works by picking and choosing elements that suit you. It's other-person centered. It's an expression of love and appreciation for the other person in the relationship. It's a humbling of yourself for the benefit of your relationship.

> *If we love our Christian brothers and sisters, it proves that we have passed from death to life. But a person who has no love is still dead. Anyone who hates another brother or sister is really a murderer at heart. And you know that murderers don't have eternal life within them.*
>
> *~ 1 John 3:14-15*

When you don't repent, you're sowing (planting, giving) hatred and death to the person you wronged. Not only are you killing the relationship, you are killing a part of them. Visualize it this way: whatever part of you overlaps with the person you wronged is now dead in both of you. The only way to bring that part of you both back to life is to repent. The above passage from *1 John 3* states so simply and eloquently, *if you love someone, you have passed from death to life, however if you have no love to give, you are still dead.* The dead cannot give life; death only reaps more death.

Fortunately for us all, God made a way for us to choose life every day, in every situation, in all of our relationships. We can choose to love and receive love. We can choose to repent and accept repentant acts. We can choose to forgive and accept forgiveness. Those are choices for life. When we choose *not* to love, repent or forgive, we are willfully choosing death.

David understood this and appealed to God's love for him when he repented. He sought to restore life to himself through love.

> *Have mercy on me, O God, because of Your unfailing love. Because of Your great compassion, blot out the stain of my sins.*
>
> *~ Psalm 51:1*

Those who love have a desire to relieve the suffering of their loved ones. Their compassion gives them an awareness of the distress their loved one is feeling. Through love, they are able to see the repentant heart reaching out to them, and they are able to reach back to alleviate it. The Word tells us in *1 Corinthians 13:7* that love never fails.

> *Love never gives up, never loses faith, is always hopeful, and endures through every circumstance.*

Right there you have it! Love will survive anything and everything. We have to allow it to work when we are given the opportunity to do so. In other words, love is never going to be the issue; how we process it and apply it will determine rather we succeed or fail in our relationships.

Further in his appeal to love in *Psalm 51:9*, David says,

> *Don't keep looking at my sins. Remove the stain of my guilt.*

He is asking for absolution. It's direct and clear. Again, *1 Corinthians 13:5* supports his request,

> *Love keeps no record of being wronged.*

When you allow love to work in your relationships, it is only a matter of time before complete healing manifests. Healing is initiated when the party responsible for causing offense repents for the wrongs they committed in the relationship.

David wasn't done. He continued in *Psalm 51:12-13*,

> *Restore to me the joy of Your salvation, and make me willing to obey You. Then I will teach Your ways to rebels, and they will return to You.*

He brings to God's remembrance their former relationship. He had been happy! He had joyfully basked in the salvation of his Lord. He wanted that back. *Give it back to me, please,* he's asking. And he doesn't stop there. He asks for assistance in keeping on track. He is aware of his imperfections. He's not trying to act as if he will never be tempted again. He's asking to be held accountable in a loving manner. *Make me willing to obey you.* Think about that....

Has anyone ever forgiven you, and then ignored you? Or forgiven you and then treated you harshly? While at the same time expecting you to keep the promises you made to them when you repented? How difficult was it to keep your promise?

Now think of a time when someone has forgiven you and never mentioned your transgression again. The love flowed freely between the two of you. How easy was it to keep the promises you made when you repented?

These are rather simplistic examples, but you should get the idea. Nothing in a relationship is about just one person – though many people go through great effort to make it seem so. Every interaction in a relationship has a double-sided effect. How we respond is equally as important as what was initiated and how it was initiated. In other words, you may not be the cause of a difficult situation, but how you respond will have as much impact on how your relationship survives that difficulty as the person who caused the offense.

David wraps up his prayer of repentance, his direct appeal to God, with:

> *The sacrifice You desire is a broken spirit. You will not reject a broken and repentant heart, O God.*
> *~Psalm 51:17*

Again, what we learn explicitly about love in *1 Corinthians 13:6* is,

> *Love does not rejoice about injustice but rejoices whenever the truth wins out.*

Why is honesty in relationships so difficult? I don't know if there's any one answer, but since Adam and Eve fell from grace in the Garden, people have been hiding their true selves as much as possible, whenever possible. It's only when we come clean, bare all, open up and be true to ourselves and to others that we experience the true joy of love rejoicing for us. Love is never going to be happy in the midst of wrong. But love will always rejoice when the wrong is made right. David was so secure in God's love for him that he appealed to that *love* knowing God would not reject him when he humbled himself completely and addressed all his wrongdoing.

Did you know David was completely forgiven? Not only was he forgiven, but God held him up as an example of what He was looking for in mankind. How is that so? David's story is full of war and sex and an arrogance that comes from repeated triumphs due to God's favor. His sin against God was adultery. God had blessed David's life so much that David got to a point of thinking that God's laws no longer applied to him. He saw a woman he wanted, took her and had her husband killed. These are the sins David is repenting for in *Psalm 51*.

David is on God's list of favorites because he loved his Lord and praised Him, he loved God's laws, he studied the word, he prayed, he sang, he worshipped. The cherry on top – David repented when he became aware of his sin! Every time. Deeply and wholeheartedly. His intention was to remain in right standing with God all his life. When he failed, he acknowledged his failure and pleaded for forgiveness. We all fall short, it's in our DNA. The truest proof of our character is how we correct our mistakes.

The prophet Nathan confronted David about his sins against God with a very eloquent parable. David was convicted with awareness of his grievous wrongs and immediately acknowledged his actions as sins against God. Just as quickly, God forgave him. The conversation is in *2 Samuel 12:1-14*.

> *So the LORD sent Nathan the prophet to tell David this story: "There were two men in a certain town. One was rich, and one was poor. The rich man owned a great many sheep and cattle. The poor man owned nothing but one little lamb he had bought. He raised that little lamb, and it grew up with his children. It ate from the man's own plate and drank from his cup. He cuddled it in his arms like a baby daughter. One day a guest arrived at the home of the rich man. But instead of killing an animal from his own flock or herd, he took the poor man's lamb and killed it and prepared it for his guest."*
>
> *David was furious. "As surely as the LORD lives," he vowed, "any man who would do such a thing*

deserves to die! He must repay four lambs to the poor man for the one he stole and for having no pity."

Then Nathan said to David, "You are that man! The LORD, the God of Israel, says: I anointed you king of Israel and saved you from the power of Saul. I gave you your master's house and his wives and the kingdoms of Israel and Judah. And if that had not been enough, I would have given you much, much more. Why, then, have you despised the word of the LORD and done this horrible deed? For you have murdered Uriah the Hittite with the sword of the Ammonites and stolen his wife. From this time on, your family will live by the sword because you have despised me by taking Uriah's wife to be your own.

"This is what the LORD says: Because of what you have done, I will cause your own household to rebel against you. I will give your wives to another man before your very eyes, and he will go to bed with them in public view. You did it secretly, but I will make this happen to you openly in the sight of all Israel."

Then David confessed to Nathan, "I have sinned against the LORD."

Nathan replied, "Yes, but the LORD has forgiven you, and you won't die for this sin. Nevertheless, because you have shown utter contempt for the LORD by doing this, your child will die."

Do you see how God followed His own process? Nathan the prophet was His mouthpiece. Nathan was sent directly to David to confront him with his sin. Isn't it interesting how David saw the sin immediately when he thought Nathan was talking about someone else? We're still like that, aren't we? We can identify everyone else's faults long before we see our own. But Nathan was emphatic: *"You are the man I'm talking about!"* Then Nathan proceeded to pronounce God's judgment on David right there. David immediately acknowledged and confessed his sin against God. Nathan then replied, *"Ok, God forgives you and you may live. However, you will reap the consequences of your actions."*

Just because you repent and are forgiven does not mean that there are no consequences. You will still have to face the consequences of your actions. Remember that.

Had David's punishment been up to him, he would have died on the spot. A sinner's judgment can be harsh! Thank God for His loving compassion!

The first thing David uttered after hearing Nathan's story was that such a man deserved to die. Spiritually, he had died because God was not with him in His sin. This is such a glaring example of what happens to interpersonal relationships when there's a huge offense separating the two parties. Each party is able to see the other person's transgression so clearly and barely have awareness of their own. Until the person who caused offense steps up to say, "I am the one at fault, what can I do to make amends" the relationship will remain fractured and the parties will remain separated. Repentance leads to life – when you repent in your interpersonal relationships you breathe life into them.

Why Repent?

People who conceal their sins will not prosper, but if they confess and turn from them, they will receive mercy. Blessed are those who fear to do wrong, but the stubborn are headed for serious trouble.
Proverbs 28:13-14

Bare-bones truth: you need to repent so you can be forgiven. God wants to forgive you. Your loved one wants to forgive you. And you want to be forgiven. That's truly all you need to know, but I will share some verses to encourage you in expressing your repentance because you are responsible for breathing life into your relationships.

God wants you to be free. Not only that, he wants you to prosper in your freedom. When you conceal your sin, cover up your wrong, or hide from your victim, you are putting and keeping yourself in bondage.

Acts 2:38-39 outlines the process of repentance, forgiveness and the promise of grace.

> *Each of you must repent of your sins and turn to God, and be baptized in the name of Jesus Christ for the forgiveness of your sins. Then you will receive the gift of the Holy Spirit. This promise is to you, and to your children, and even to the Gentiles — all who have been called by the Lord our God."*

I would like to translate this for modern ears and interpersonal relationships: *Each of you must feel sorry (contrite or regretful for your past conduct) and turn away from your wrong ways to face the person you harmed. Cleanse (purge, purify) yourself in order to receive the forgiveness you seek. You will then be graced with mercy. When you receive it, you will be changed.*

When you are truly repentant, your heart changes. A heart change precipitates changes in your thoughts, which are followed by changes in your behavior. You then completely stop and turn away from the actions for which you have repented. You do an about-face. You are changed through your repentance. The improved you is in a better position to improve your relationship with the person you hurt.

Repentance is a step in our individual spiritual growth process. When you refuse to repent, you are in effect stunting your growth. You won't be able to see much beyond the situation you're stuck in.

Repent and receive the blessing of life to your relationships and your spiritual life.

Repentance Leads to Healing

Oh, what joy for those whose disobedience is forgiven, whose sin is put out of sight! Yes, what joy for those whose record the LORD has cleared of guilt, whose lives are lived in complete honesty!
When I refused to confess my sin, my body wasted away, and I groaned all day long. Day and night Your hand of discipline was heavy on me. My strength evaporated like water in the summer heat.
Finally, I confessed all my sins to You and stopped trying to hide my guilt. I said to myself, "I will confess my rebellion to the LORD."
And You forgave me! All my guilt is gone.
Psalm 32:1-5

The problem with free will is that we are born with a certain amount of arrogance, which grows exponentially depending on our exposures and experiences. Two fruit of that arrogance are a sense of entitlement and a belief that you can do no wrong. The idea that you are better than others also manifests from that root of pride.

When your way conflicts with someone else's and you knowingly persist on your course to their detriment, you are in the wrong. When your words are maliciously spoken, even with a measure of truth, you are wrong. When you apologize only to get over a rough spot, but you really don't mean it, you're still wrong. Life isn't about having everything your way, saying exactly what you want, however you want, and blowing kisses to smooth over ruffled feathers.

Speaking words of remorse and actually feeling so remorseful for your actions that you change your ways are two separate things. Anyone can apologize for a wrong and ask for forgiveness. But the truly repentant are recognized by the changes they make in their life after they repent.

> *Prove by the way you live that you have repented of your sins and turned to God. Don't just say to each other, 'We're safe, for we are descendants of Abraham.' That means nothing, for I tell you, God can create children of Abraham from these very stones. Even now the ax of God's judgment is poised, ready to sever the roots of the trees. Yes, every tree that does not produce good fruit will be chopped down and thrown into the fire."*
>
> ~ Luke 3:8-9

Skip and demand does not restore

Skipping the step of repenting for a wrong you committed and demanding to be forgiven for your behavior does not heal the fracture and restore the relationship to its former status or allow it to move forward. It actually causes more damage.

> *"Therefore, I will judge each of you, O people of Israel, according to your actions," says the Sovereign LORD. "Repent, and turn from your sins. Don't let them destroy you! Put all your rebellion behind you, and find yourselves a new heart and a new spirit. For why should you die, O people of Israel? I don't want you to die," says the Sovereign LORD. "Turn back and live!"*
>
> ~ Ezekiel 18:30-32

We always have the choice of life. Every day. Every decision. Every relationship. We can consciously make decisions and take actions that will either support our relationships or damage them. We all want healthy relationships; however, we don't always choose to do things that represent life in them.

If you are confronted by a loved one about a perceived wrong, from their perspective, that you disagree with, do not argue with them about their perception. In a very true sense, perception is reality. It's an individual's view of the world and how they fit into it. If someone's perception is that you hurt them, no matter what you say in your defense, they are still hurt. Making excuses for your behavior doesn't take the hurt away. Suggesting that they brought the hurt unto themselves will only compound the pain and widen gulf in the relationship. The best thing to do is to acknowledge that their pain is real, even though you may not have had any intention of causing it. Make amends for whatever harm you caused. That action, that expression of care and concern would most likely remove the pain, after which full recovery is only a matter of time.

Refusing to repent works against love and forgiveness.

You don't need to apologize for anything you didn't do or say, but if you did say or do something that harmed someone, take responsibility for your words and actions and express what your intentions were.

If you cause harm and your way of dealing with the repercussions is to guilt the person you harmed into forgiving you and forgetting about the situation, then in essence you are devaluing the other person, their feelings and your relationship with them.

The injured person may be willing to forgive you but unable to do so if you aren't repentant. If that's the case their best recourse is to give the situation to the Father and ask that He forgives you for your offense against them.

> *People who conceal their sins will not prosper, but if they confess and turn from them, they will receive mercy.*
>
> *~ Proverbs 28:13*

Repent and hope for forgiveness

Unfortunately, popular culture is extremely accepting of so many vices and deviant behaviors that people attuned to cultural things have an *expectation* to be forgiven for their offenses (which aren't as bad as the next person's, by the way!). These people are only familiar with the propaganda associated with forgiveness – the popular teachings by the popular preachers and the social practices exhibited by celebrities. Most people know the bottom line: forgiveness is the correct choice. These people will play on the offended person's sense of morality, suggesting that the person they offended is in the wrong because they're holding a grudge or that they are hindering the progress of the relationship by withholding their immediate forgiveness. People like this may not even consider humbling themselves and offering to make amends for the harm they caused.

Repentance is perhaps the most crucial step in the process of forgiveness. Without it, the relationship remains broken. Repentance heals and cleanses the offender. The healing and cleansing then flow from the offender through the relationship connection to the offended party.

> *When I refused to confess my sin, my body wasted away, and I groaned all day long. Day and night your*

> hand of discipline was heavy on me. My strength evaporated like water in the summer heat.
>
> ~ Psalm 32:3-4

People who are aware of their error, yet refuse to take corrective actions, are consumed with guilt. It may not show outwardly, but internally they are destroying themselves. When you refuse to admit to your wrongdoing and repent for it, you bring death to your body and your relationship. In *Psalm 32*, David eloquently expresses the disaster he brought to his physical body when he refused to repent. He didn't just say he felt "guilty," he described the physical manifestations of his guilt – a weakened, wasted body heavy with depression.

David didn't expect to be forgiven. He had no hope of receiving it. He became so depressed and worn down that he had no energy to hide from his wrongdoing. He had no more interest in lying. He was so weak he went to his source of strength and exposed himself. *"This is what I did,"* he said. *"This is how I rebelled against you. I don't know what to do. I don't know how to make it right, but I am taking responsibility for my actions. I am admitting to my willful disobedience. I acknowledge my arrogance and pride. Yes, I took advantage of those you placed in my care. Yes, I spoke against those you sent to sharpen me. Regretfully, I treated some of your creation hatefully. I am so very sorry, Lord!"*

By the time David got to the point of supplicating himself to the Lord, he was probably only seeking to unload his burden of guilt. His heartfelt repentance was rewarded by God's forgiveness of his sin.

> *The sacrifice You desire is a broken spirit. You will not reject a broken and repentant heart, O God.*
>
> Psalm 51:16-17

Forgiveness is a reward. Not a right. And it's only truly possible through the grace of God.

David didn't understand that until he experienced it. He was free to live in the open with truth and honesty again. He was free to seek and enjoy God without shame. David knew God loved him. His life was a testament to God's favor on him. But it wasn't until David sinned against God and had to make it right that he realized the only way to repair his relationship with God was by exposing himself, opening himself, giving himself completely to the Lord. David's contrite (penitent) heart was all God needed to forgive him his sin. After he repented, forgiveness was offered and the relationship was restored.

David begins *Psalm 32* with joy:

> *Oh, what joy for those whose disobedience is forgiven, whose sin is put out of sight!*

The New International Version translates the first two verses of *Psalm 32* this way:

> *Blessed is he whose transgressions are forgiven, whose sins are covered. Blessed is the man whose sin the LORD does not count against him and in whose spirit is no deceit.*

When you repent, you allow love to work its perfect work and cover the violations you committed in your relationship. Love spreads over, wraps up, protects, shields, compensates, makes up for everything else – when you repent. Love doesn't cover and hide your transgressions as if in shame. No, love spreads over and puts your sin away. In the covering it operates as a bridge for the offended party to walk towards you as well and bless you by offering their open heart in forgiveness. Love is the healer.

The Benefit of Repentance

When you were slaves to sin, you were free from the obligation to do right. And what was the result? You are now ashamed of the things you used to do, things that end in eternal doom. But now you are free from the power of sin and have become slaves of God. Now you do those things that lead to holiness and result in eternal life. For the wages of sin is death, but the free gift of God is eternal life through Christ Jesus our Lord.
Romans 6:20-23

I'm in a season of sifting and cleansing. God has completely stripped me of all my most influential and intimate relationships. All the "excellent" friends I once thought I could depend on for anything at anytime – gone. The family members who would "die" for me weren't interested in sharing "life" with me. The friends and family who are still in contact are so emotionally and spiritually distant it's like speaking to an acquaintance at an annual workplace conference when we do connect throughout the year. We no longer have much in common and our paths rarely cross.

When God first started stripping me five years ago (that's when I noticed anyway), I fought against it, of course. I had no idea what was going on spiritually, but I knew that in my physical life I didn't want to lose my friendships or my family. So I reached out and tried to grab them back. I asked if I had caused offense, if there was anything I could help them with. I asked if we could spend time together. But those relationships had never been about what I wanted. Yet, I was in recovery mode. I was willing to do whatever I needed to do to maintain and improve the relationships I had. I was repenting and hadn't done anything wrong – or at least nothing that anyone was willing to speak to me about. It didn't matter to me whose fault it was that our relationship began to falter, I was willing to take responsibility for them all in the hope of healing the breaches. As time went on, I realized I was working against God's plan for me. How did I come to that conclusion? My efforts to rehabilitate produced no fruit. It doesn't take long to see results when you're working with God.

I realized my season had changed and people were being moved out of my life to achieve His purpose. When I stopped fighting against this transition, I was able to see clearer and understand better. I was able to recognize God's work even in the process of manifestation. I became able to review situations and ask, "What is the benefit of keeping this relationship in my life? Will I really miss its absence?" The answers were "none" and "no" to the relationships He stripped from me. I couldn't see that by myself. I thought *love* was in those relationships. I thought support was there. Camaraderie. Shelter. Comfort. Shoulders to cry on. Hugs to lean into. People to whom I could show myself to. Everything I have come to rely on God for I was relying on my friends and family for. I didn't understand the ramifications then, but I was putting all my other relationships before my relationship with God.

> *Be very careful never to make a treaty with the people who live in the land where you are going. If you do, you will follow their evil ways and be trapped. You must*

> *worship no other gods, for the* LORD, *whose very name is Jealous, is a God who is jealous about His relationship with you.*
>
> ~Exodus 34:12, 14

When we place anything or anyone before God, we sin in each instance. I recognize and appreciate that He stripped me of everything that took my focus off of Him. By and large, nothing and no one has been removed from me that damaged me upon its removal. As a matter of fact, with each removal I felt a distinct sense of relief – as if a weight had been lifted from me. The relationships I was freed from were good or decent by the world's standards, but by Kingdom standards they weren't benefitting me at all. They didn't edify or encourage me in my spirit or faith at all. Therefore, I was holding on to relationships that were not bearing fruit – they were spiritually dead.

I must make an important distinction. All of our relationships fall into one of two categories – godly or worldly. Our godly (Kingdom) relationships will have a foundation of shared belief and faith systems. Our worldly relationships will not have that shared foundation at all. On the surface, practicing the process of love, repentance and forgiveness will work wherever applied. However, Kingdom practices multiply fruit exponentially in Kingdom relationships. Why? Because both parties are applying the same principles.

When a Believer practices the Word of God in a relationship with a nonbeliever, it's possible the Believer will not be around to see the Word manifest in the nonbeliever's life. As *Exodus 34:12* instructs, we are to be careful with whom we associate. It is equally as likely for the nonbeliever to negatively influence the Believer as it is for the Believer to positively influence the nonbeliever. So

Believers need to get used to planting, watering or shining light – whatever is necessary wherever we are – then be prepared to move on. We should not get so entrenched that we attempt to stay present for the whole growth season for every nonbeliever we encounter. God is going to protect His own with limited exposure to those operating outside of His will. Listen to His promptings.

Are you a slave to sin or a slave of God?

> *Now you do those things that lead to holiness and result in eternal life. For the wages of sin is death, but the free gift of God is eternal life through Christ Jesus our Lord.*
>
> ~ Romans 6:22-23

Romans 6:20-21 tells us that before we repent to God we are slaves to sin with no obligation to do right. That lack of obligation should not be mistaken for freedom. It is not. It allows you to do things that will lead you directly to eternal death.

When we accept Jesus Christ as our Lord and Savior, we free ourselves from the power of sin and enslave ourselves to God's will. Our *willing* submission to God leads to holiness and eternal life (v.22).

So, I ask, what is the ultimate benefit of repentance?

Answer: Life.

What you learn in your relationship with God is one hundred percent transferrable to all your earthly relationships, which are a microcosm of what God wants us to learn for our spiritual life.

The Importance of Repentance

"As surely as I live," says the Sovereign LORD.... "All people are mine to judge — both parents and children alike. And this is my rule: The person who sins is the one who will die.

"Therefore, I will judge each of you, O people of Israel, according to your actions," says the Sovereign LORD.

"Repent, and turn from your sins. Don't let them destroy you! Put all your rebellion behind you, and find yourselves a new heart and a new spirit. For why should you die, O people of Israel? I don't want you to die," says the Sovereign LORD. "Turn back and live!"

Ezekiel 18:3-4, 30-32

We have already explored what repentance is, why we should repent and the benefit of repentance. Now we will review why it's so important.

Repentance is the foundational stone of God's law for His people. Repentance is the reason God came to Earth in the human form of Jesus Christ. Jesus's purpose was to die for our sins – He repented for us. More explicitly, Jesus repented for the original sin Adam committed in the Garden of Eden. Adam never repented. Because of his disobedience, everyone descended from him (i.e. all of mankind) inherited his sin. Jesus came to remove that sin debt from mankind. Through His death, we all have access to eternal life.

So you see, just as death came into the world through a man, now the resurrection from the dead has begun through another man. Just as everyone dies because we all belong to Adam, everyone who belongs to Christ will be given new life.

~ 1 Corinthians 15:21-22

Life and death revolve around your willingness to repent.

How plaintive is our Dear Father in Heaven's plea to us? *"Why do you choose to die, my children, my chosen, my loved ones? I don't want you to die! Come back to me and live!" (Ezekiel 18:31-32)*

Turn back to me and live.

When we do wrong, we are not facing God. In order to be free of the power of sin we must literally turn away from the sin we are committing and face God. God is in one direction, death is in the opposite direction.

Relationship application

When you commit a wrong in a relationship and do not repent (correct the wrong) you are planting death in that relationship. The longer you go without repenting the more time and opportunity death has to spread throughout that relationship and perhaps others. Meaning, all your wrongs will begin to accumulate.

You need to be aware of your words and actions and how aligned they are with your promises and follow-through. If you want a relationship to thrive, you need to be able to acknowledge when you are wrong and repent for any harm you cause. The more you sincerely repent in your interpersonal relationships, the more you breathe life into them.

Just as God doesn't want any of us to die, in most cases, we don't want our interpersonal relationships to die either. Not the ones we were born into (family) or the ones we discover on our journey (friends). We have no say in our family connections, but we spend a great deal of our lives trying to maintain and improve various familial relationships. When we choose our friends we choose people who remind us of ourselves, thereby occasionally making the mistaken assumption that less effort is needed to maintain and improve those relationships.

Relationship matters. The import isn't necessarily on the type of relationship, because important lessons will be learned from all relationships. Here's something to remember as a key relationship maintenance key: you are only forgiven up to your last episode of repentance. The nature of mankind is to fall and get back up. We're still here because when we get back to our feet, we are better off than we were when we fell down. Recovering from our failings actually improves us. Making amends for breaking a vase on Monday won't cover the hole you kick into the wall on Wednesday. You have to repent for each wrong and the effects they have on the other person in the relationship – whether intentional or not.

Dealing with the Unrepentant

*Sin whispers to the wicked, deep within their hearts.
They have no fear of God at all. In their blind conceit,
they cannot see how wicked they really are. Everything
they say is crooked and deceitful. They refuse to act
wisely or do good. They lie awake at night, hatching
sinful plots. Their actions are never good. They make
no attempt to turn from evil.*
Psalm 36:1-4

One of the saddest truths we will ever have to face is: *not everyone is for us*. No matter how much we may love someone and want them to share in our lives, their presence in our life may be toxic. Toxic relationships destroy life.

Sometimes we want people in our life who have no interest in treating us well. They plot and scheme for their own advantage with no consideration for the destruction they leave in their path – usually in your life.

Though the overall message of the Bible is very euphoric – we are loved so much we can't comprehend or explain it outside of Biblical terms – the nuts and bolts of the message is realistically gritty. We need to pay attention to the nuts and bolts and trust in the overall to get us through.

Matthew 10:31 tells us every sin (transgression, offense) committed on Earth is forgivable.

> *"So I tell you, every sin and blasphemy can be forgiven — except blasphemy against the Holy Spirit, which will never be forgiven. Anyone who speaks against the Son of Man can be forgiven, but anyone who speaks against the Holy Spirit will never be forgiven, either in this world or in the world to come.*
>
> ~ Matthew 10:31-32

Please note the passage does not say that every sin *will be* forgiven. It says clearly that every sin *can be* – meaning, it's possible to forgive anything. What has to happen to bring forgiveness about? That's the overall message. The nuts and bolts are in the process. The feelings associated with the offense, communicating those feelings, and healing from those feelings. The process takes time, but forgiveness is always possible.

An example of an easy flow process would be: offense happens => offended confronts offender => offender acknowledges wrong and make amends => offended accepts apology and offers forgiveness (debt paid in full). That's a process that anyone, who has worked through it, knows takes longer than the two seconds it took to read about it.

The unrepentant, however, changes the flow of the process to look more like: offense happens => offended confronts offender => offender denies accusation or refuses to acknowledge wrong and make amends => offended retreats, feeling more hurt => offended asks for help from mutual friends or family => offender is even more forceful in denials => offended is hurt even more => [if grounded in the Word] offended asks God to forgive offender and to heal the pain in their heart => original offense is now between offender and God.

When you have done all you can do, you hand the unrepentant person over to God. God sees all and knows all. He is patient and His justice is eternal.

Don't allow people to destroy you. Don't give anyone that power over your life. If someone is sowing death (destruction, discord, anger, hatred, etc.) into your life and into your relationship with them, walk away – after you have done everything you know to do based on God's instructions. If we become unwilling to forgive because of someone else's refusal to repent, then we are sinning. When you are unwilling to forgive, you are choosing death. Save yourself, choose life, and leave the unrepentant to God.

You've Repented. Now What?

But while knowledge makes us feel important, it is love that strengthens the church. Anyone who claims to know all the answers doesn't really know very much. But the person who loves God is the one whom God recognizes.
1 Corinthians 8:1-3

Acknowledge the effort and process of giving and receiving repentance and forgiveness.

Learn from your mistakes and correct your behavior. If your relationships remain intact, they will be stronger. If you truly learn from the estrangement your offense precipitates, you will not allow such offenses to occur again. And if the offended persons have learned from the episodes, they will be wiser in their dealings with you. Meaning, they will avoid doing anything to encourage your prior wrongdoings.

Overall, your interactions will reveal love in a deeper and stronger way. You'll have a real-life example of love's endurance and how love flourishes when you don't seek your own way and interests in your relationships.

On the other hand, it's a harsh reality that a repentant heart is not always well received. If the relationship is not restored after you've repented, that's okay. The relationship may be lost, but the lesson doesn't have to be! Take note of your life and your experiences. Learn your lessons from every interaction and relationship. You can be assured that whatever lessons you miss will come back around at a later date in a similar, though more intense, situation. Save yourself heartache and additional pain – learn all you can the first time and apply your knowledge going forward.

Give thanks for the relationship and the opportunity of having that person in your life, and move on. Grow forward. Never regret your repentance. Repenting for your offenses make you right with God, no matter what response you receive from the person you offended. It's great to save the relationship, but your Father in Heaven appreciates you saving yourself (through the way He provided) much more! This process will edify you in your walk with the Lord, no matter how the situation turns out.

> *But you, dear friends, must build each other up in your most holy faith, pray in the power of the Holy Spirit, and await the mercy of our Lord Jesus Christ, who will bring you eternal life. In this way, you will keep yourselves safe in God's love.*
>
> *~ Jude 1:20-21*

The Relationship Between Repentance & Forgiveness

I am not sorry that I sent that severe letter to you, though I was sorry at first, for I know it was painful to you for a little while. Now I am glad I sent it, not because it hurt you, but because the pain caused you to repent and change your ways. It was the kind of sorrow God wants His people to have, so you were not harmed by us in any way. For the kind of sorrow God wants us to experience leads us away from sin and results in salvation. There's no regret for that kind of sorrow. But worldly sorrow, which lacks repentance, results in spiritual death.

Just see what this godly sorrow produced in you! Such earnestness, such concern to clear yourselves, such indignation, such alarm, such longing to see me, such zeal, and such a readiness to punish wrong. You showed that you have done everything necessary to make things right. My purpose, then, was not to write about who did the wrong or who was wronged. I wrote to you so that in the sight of God you could see for yourselves how loyal you are to us. We have been greatly encouraged by this.

2 Corinthians 7:8-13

Is forgiveness really possible without repentance?

No, not by yourself. You can choose to ignore or overlook an offense committed against you, but that's different than forgiving the same offense.

Before studying for, researching and writing this book, I believed what I was taught in church about "unforgiveness" being a sin. "Unforgiveness" happens when someone doesn't forgive an offender that hasn't asked for forgiveness or repented for their offense and is taught to be a sin itself. According to some teachings I've heard, in order to avoid the sin of "unforgiveness," one must forgive all transgressions committed against them, whether the offender wants it or not. We are sometimes instructed to forgive even when the offender hasn't acknowledged their wrong in any way; even the most unrepentant offenders. Why? Reasons vary, but the primary theory is to obtain freedom. By forgiving unilaterally, one would then be released from the hurt caused by the offender and would not be prone to bitterness, resentment, hatred and other self-destructive emotions.

It sounds very noble and self-edifying, but it's not scriptural.

I have since learned that "unforgiveness" is not a word mentioned in the Bible at all; it sounds Biblical, but has no Biblical weight. Those who teach about "unforgiveness" imply that the offended person is stubbornly holding on to their hurts, and should offer blanket forgiveness. Rarely is the process of forgiveness outlined or discussed during these teachings.

What the preachers of "unforgiveness" are perhaps drawing from, is the fact that our original sin was forgiven when Christ died on the cross. However, the new sins we commit in our relationships or after accepting salvation are not covered by Christ's sacrifice. Those are issues we have to work through here and now. Yet, we are able to forgive anything and everything that comes against us *because* of the grace we received through Christ's physical death on the cross. If you operate in scripture, this is how you can forgive others as God forgives you. It's possible through God's grace.

Repentance is a key element in the forgiveness process. Without it, forgiveness is not possible on our own. The process of forgiveness requires bilateral effort from the person causing offense and the person on the receiving end of the offense. Nowhere in the Bible are we told that anyone is forgiven without first repenting. Therefore, in order for someone to be graced with forgiveness, they must first humble themselves and repent for their offense(s).

Alternatively, when repentance is not offered, the offended has the option to release the offender to God. You can ask God to forgive them for their sin against you. You are interceding on their behalf and in the process releasing yourself from the hurt caused by the offense. By seeking God and His mercy and grace upon the offender, you are freeing yourself of any roots of bitterness, anger, resentment and hatred. More importantly, you are expressing your *willingness* to forgive when you hand the situation over to God.

Repentance is so important that when the offender does not repent, the relationship does not recover. Even when the offended party hands the situation over to God and even if the two parties continue to function within the relationship, they aren't able to get past the emotional barrier the offense creates. That barrier could represent a broken trust, a lack of faith, a fear of future hurt, a shutdown in communication or any number of expressions of emotional pain. Whatever the barrier and however it manifests in the relationship, it will not begin to crumble until the offender turns away from wrongdoing, stops hurtful activity, corrects what they are able to correct and make amends for everything that led to the barrier being erected. If that full repentance is not forthcoming, then the relationship will not be fully restored.

Forgiveness

"If you forgive those who sin against you, your heavenly Father will forgive you. But if you refuse to forgive others, your Father will not forgive your sins."
Matthew 6:14-15

The Magnitude of Forgiveness

> Again He said, "Peace be with you. As the Father has sent Me, so I am sending you." Then He breathed on them and said, "Receive the Holy Spirit. If you forgive anyone's sins, they are forgiven. If you do not forgive them, they are not forgiven."
> John 20:21-23

Forgiveness is divine. It's a function of God, Jesus and the Holy Spirit. The children of God have been endowed with the ability to forgive. Meaning, we have the divine choice to forgive or not. We can offer it or withhold it. Whatever we decide, the Trinity will uphold our decision.

With great power comes great responsibility – and greater consequences. We are encouraged to offer forgiveness. Jesus tells us in *Matthew 6:14-15*:

> *If you forgive those who sin against you, your heavenly Father will forgive you. But if you refuse to forgive others, your Father will not forgive your sins.*

The prayer template that Jesus provides in *Matthew 6:9-13* subtly illustrates how forgiveness of our sins by God is conditional on our forgiveness of those who sin against us. (This should not be confused with God's love for us – His love is unconditional, however His unconditional love does not keep us from His judgment and discipline.)

> *Our Father in Heaven, may Your name be kept holy. May Your Kingdom come soon. May Your will be done on Earth, as it is in Heaven. Give us today the food we need, and forgive us our sins, as we have forgiven those who sin against us. And don't let us yield to temptation, but rescue us from the evil one.*

Forgiveness is stated simply here, but what's implied is the *process* this volume of *The MeatyWord Series* is exploring. Many Christians have sat in church and recited the words to the Lord's Prayer, as *Matthew 6:9-13* is commonly known. Many Christians have said the Lord's Prayer at the beginning of meals and prior to going to bed at night. Unfortunately, not as many Christians have taken the words in the prayer to heart or broken them down for not only true meaning, but for truer application.

> *forgive*
> 1. *to pardon an offense or an offender; absolve*
> 2. *to give up all claim on account of; remit*
> 3. *to cease to feel resentment against*
>   (Dictionary.com, 2010)

True forgiveness, fruitful forgiveness, is not possible without repentance. The fruit of forgiveness is restoration. Offering forgiveness for an offense that has not been repented is an ineffective expression of grace. It's ineffective because the graciousness will not be well received, understood or appreciated. The lack of understanding of grace directly correlates to the lack of understanding of the offense committed and its impact.

Therefore, you can only do your part when it's your turn.

That doesn't mean that we sit back and wait for the person who wronged us to come to us and repent. We should approach them and let them know what offense they committed against us. (More on this in *Forgiveness Does a Body Good*.)

Ultimately, we were created to be a reflection of God's grace and a receptacle for His love. Though Jesus speaks directly to His followers, His teachings are for us to extend to people of the world who don't know Him. Christian responsibility is two-fold, but executed from one spirit – the Holy Spirit of God. On one hand, Christians, *a.k.a.* Believers, are to encourage, correct and build up their fellows in Christ. On the other hand, Christians are to win over lost souls (those in the world) with the love God has poured into us.

Jesus was a master at illustrating His message with stories. So, I defer my Lord's words to paint a panoramic of how grace should flow from the Father (*a.k.a.* King) through His children (*a.k.a.* servants) to others (*a.k.a.* fellow servants).

> Then Peter came to him and asked, "Lord, how often should I forgive someone who sins against me? Seven times?"
>
> "No, not seven times," Jesus replied, "but seventy times seven!
>
> "Therefore, the Kingdom of Heaven can be compared to a king who decided to bring his accounts up to date with servants who had borrowed money from him. In the process, one of his debtors was brought in who owed him millions of dollars. He couldn't pay, so his master ordered that he be sold — along with his wife, his children, and everything he owned — to pay the debt.
>
> "But the man fell down before his master and begged him, 'Please, be patient with me, and I will pay it all.' Then his master was filled with pity for him, and he released him and forgave his debt.
>
> "But when the man left the king, he went to a fellow servant who owed him a few thousand dollars. He grabbed him by the throat and demanded instant payment.

> "His fellow servant fell down before him and begged for a little more time. 'Be patient with me, and I will pay it,' he pleaded. But his creditor wouldn't wait. He had the man arrested and put in prison until the debt could be paid in full.
>
> "When some of the other servants saw this, they were very upset. They went to the king and told him everything that had happened. Then the king called in the man he had forgiven and said, 'You evil servant! I forgave you that tremendous debt because you pleaded with me. Shouldn't you have mercy on your fellow servant, just as I had mercy on you?' Then the angry king sent the man to prison to be tortured until he had paid his entire debt.
>
> "That's what my heavenly Father will do to you if you refuse to forgive your brothers and sisters from your heart."
>
> ~ Matthew 18:21-35

What a powerful story!

Notice how the king did not forgive the servant's debt *until after* the servant humbled himself before him? Forgiveness is not automatic just because you stand in the presence of the king! We have to humble ourselves. And forgiveness doesn't automatically flow through us. We have to willfully offer it to others after they have humbled themselves for their transgressions against us.

In the parable, "humble" is representative of "repentance," but it reaches beyond a one-time action. It's a willful act of subjecting oneself to another's will and acknowledging their authority.

The king called the first servant evil because he didn't follow the king's example. God has provided us with an instruction manual describing His expectations. It's up to us to *choose* to obey. That's it; that's our only real choice. Intellectually, we stumble on the belief that we have been gifted with the option of free will. Our ego expands on the practice of doing what we want, when we want, and how we want. Realistically, *every* decision we make on earth is only truly between two options set before us from the beginning of creation: life and death.

> *"Now listen! Today I am giving you a choice between life and death, between prosperity and disaster. For I command you this day to love the LORD your God and to keep His commands, decrees, and regulations by walking in His ways. If you do this, you will live and multiply, and the LORD your God will bless you and the land you are about to enter and occupy.*
>
> *"But if your heart turns away and you refuse to listen (obey), and if you are drawn away to serve and worship other gods, then I warn you now that you will certainly be destroyed. You will not live a long, good life in the land you are crossing the Jordan to occupy.*
>
> *"Today I have given you the choice between life and death, between blessings and curses. Now I call on Heaven and Earth to witness the choice you make. Oh, that you would choose life, so that you and your descendants might live! You can make this choice by loving the LORD your God, obeying Him, and committing yourself firmly to Him. This is the key to your life.*
>
> ~ *Deuteronomy 30:15-20*

I love how the proclamations and instructions in this passage begin with "today." The choice between life and death is a choice we make every day. It's not a "one time" thing. Walking in the Lord's ways takes daily commitment, decision by decision. When we obey God, follow His examples, accept His sacrifice and adhere to His greatest commandment (love God first with everything in us), we then choose life. When we disobey or reject Him *at any point,* we are then choosing death.

God wants to bless and prosper us; however He has given us the option to choose death and destruction. It doesn't sound fair, but fairness as we think of it, isn't a Biblical principle.

That has to be sobering for you! It certainly is for me. So, the issue with forgiveness is that God has given us a template. We simply have to follow it. He forgave us first because Jesus humbled Himself in our place. God was able to forgive us because Jesus repented for Adam's sin (which all of Adam's seed has inherited). Jesus died once to save us from spiritual death always. The memory of Adam's disobedience may not be in your physical memory, but that doesn't mean that you are exempt from the consequences of his actions. We are all physically born into sin (disobedience, death, separation from God). Our spiritual birth (obedience, life, unity with God) happens when we accept Jesus Christ as our Lord and Savior. When we accept that Jesus already *repented* for the sin we were physically born into, we acknowledge that due to His humble obedience to God's will, we have been forgiven – personally. We are the benefactors of God's sacrifice of His Son and Jesus's obedience to His Father. That forgiveness grants us a restored relationship with God. A relationship restored from the broken state Adam left it in.

Can you imagine how much Adam hurt God? Not just with his curiosity and eagerness to please his wife which led to his disobedience. Imagine how much more his *lack of repentance* pained our Heavenly Father. We experience so many difficulties in our interpersonal relationships today because Adam's unrepentant heart ruined his relationship with God. He never accepted responsibility for his actions, nor did he seek to make things right with God – his Creator, his Spirit, his Breath, his Provider, his

Father, and his Friend. Nowhere in scripture does it even hint at an attempt by Adam to even say, "I'm sorry."

Now imagine God's feelings (yes, I said feelings!) when He reflected upon Adam's disregard of His rule in the Garden – He only had one rule! He had given Adam a whole world. Literally! He populated it with creatures that Adam named. Adam was given dominion over everything on Earth. He was given a companion with whom to enjoy the experience and was encouraged to multiply and fill the Earth with his offspring. All this freedom and abundance only came with one restriction: *don't eat from the tree of the knowledge of good and evil.* The "tree of the knowledge of good and evil" is a long way of saying "death."

> *In the middle of the garden he placed the tree of life and the tree of the knowledge of good and evil.*
>
> *But the LORD God warned him, "You may freely eat the fruit of every tree in the garden — except the tree of the knowledge of good and evil. If you eat its fruit, you are sure to die."*
>
> ~ Genesis 2:9, 16-17

Once Adam ate from the tree, his fellowship with God ended. Their relationship was so damaged that God banished Adam and his wife from the paradise He had created just for them.

Going back to the story of the king forgiving his servant for the equivalent of a multi-million dollar debt, nothing anyone does to us on Earth can possibly match the original transgression against God. What the story is telling us is that since God chose to forgive *you* (it's a personal example) after Jesus repented for our mutual ancestors' offense against Him, we became obligated to forgive any offense against us when our offender repents for their transgression. If *you* choose not to forgive, then you will take on the judgment for your original debt – Adam's sin against God.

Again, you can choose life (forgiveness) or death (withhold your forgiveness).

Choose eternal life
When we accept Jesus as our Savior, we are acknowledging that He died as a sacrifice for our sins. He died so that we may have life. *First John 4:9-11* plainly states that because we Believers have already accepted and benefitted from God's love, we are to extend it to others.

> *God showed how much He loved us by sending His one and only Son into the world so that we might have eternal life through Him. This is real love — not that we loved God, but that He loved us and sent His Son as a sacrifice to take away our sins. Dear friends, since God loved us that much, we surely ought to love each other.*

In *1 John 2:12*, we are told directly that we, as children of God, are being addressed in John's letter because our sins have been forgiven through Jesus.

> *I am writing to you who are God's children because your sins have been forgiven through Jesus.*

All this grace and mercy! The cycle of love dictates that it doesn't stay in one place or with one person. Everything God gives you is meant to flow *through* you and wash over others!

Forgiveness by proxy
I don't want you to miss this because I am simply floored by it!

Jesus stood as a proxy for you and me and everyone. We can choose to accept Him as atonement for our sins.

Very simply put, a proxy is a person who has the power and authority to act as the deputy or substitute for another – an ally who can be relied upon to speak or act on one's behalf.

Jesus took our place on the cross. He stood in Adam's stead. In standing in for Adam, He stood in for you, me and everyone. Adam's sin became our sin because we were all in Adam, as seed, when he disobeyed God. Jesus acted on our behalf and repented for Adam's original sin.

Because we have been restored in fellowship and relationship with God, we have received our dominion back. We now have the authority to stand as God's proxy and offer forgiveness to those who sin against us.

> *Again He said, "Peace be with you. As the Father has sent Me, so I am sending you." Then He breathed on them and said, "Receive the Holy Spirit. If you forgive anyone's sins, they are forgiven. If you do not forgive them, they are not forgiven."*
>
> *~ John 20:21-23*

A Believer's primary goal in life should be to mirror Jesus, as He mirrors God. What this scripture is telling us is that the Spirit of God is in us when we receive Him. With that Spirit we have God's authority here on Earth. We have the Teacher (Jesus Christ), the Breath of Life (Holy Spirit) and the Power (God) to assist us in ruling our Earthly domain as God rules Heaven. We are kings who are instructed to be as gracious as the King of kings. When we fail to represent God well in our treatment of others, we reap a judgment upon ourselves that we cannot satisfy. Be careful with what you allow and disavow. When we pronounce judgment on someone on Earth, that judgment is upheld in Heaven.

> *And I will give you the keys of the Kingdom of Heaven. Whatever you forbid on Earth will be forbidden in*

> Heaven, and whatever you permit on Earth will be permitted in Heaven."
>
> ~Matthew 16:19

If we choose not to forgive after forgiveness has been sought and requested by the repentant, we are not only choosing death for ourselves, we are choosing death for someone else. We are hindering a fellow brother's or sister's progress. We are withholding life from them when we choose not to forgive. In His wrath, God is saying, *"I have forgiven you for so much! How can you not forgive this person for so little?"*

We are effectively tying God's hands for particular sins against us, because we stand as His proxy when forgiveness is requested and we refuse to give it. We are then guilty of representing our loving Father as an unforgiving God, lacking in compassion.

Another way of looking at this is: you go to God on your knees and ask that He forgive you for missing church last Sunday. Perhaps it was the first service you missed in five years and you didn't think it would be a problem. You apologize and offer to make up for the offense, but God withholds His forgiveness and sends you to hell until He feels your lapse has been properly atoned for. That sounds like a very powerful punishment for something seemingly insignificant in the whole scheme of things.

Well, that is what God is telling us through Jesus. Anything we consider a major transgression here on Earth is insignificant compared to the original sin against God. Since He has forgiven His children their collective original sin, there is no reason for His children to hold on to any sin committed against them when the transgressor has repented.

More importantly, there are severe consequences when we, as proxies, do something contrary to what God Himself would do.

Forgiveness Does the Body Good

A peaceful heart leads to a healthy body; jealousy is like cancer in the bones.
Proverbs 14:30

Forgiveness is an element of love. It's one of love's characteristics. You really can't have true love in you and be unforgiving. That doesn't mean that forgiveness is easy. Or immediate. It's a process. Going through the process of forgiving someone does more good for you than them, but ultimately, it brings restoration and health to relationships.

When we hold grudges, pain, bitterness, resentment, hurt, anger or any other negative feeling against someone for their treatment of us, we are internalizing all that negativity. We're keeping it captive within our body, our mind, our spirit. It grows within us in such a way that it changes how we see the world, how we treat others, how we express emotion, how we interact in society. It changes how we accept God and interact with Him. It minimizes our ability to love.

Jesus outlines the process of forgiveness in *Matthew 18:15-17:*

> *"If another believer sins against you, go privately and point out the offense. If the other person listens and confesses it, you have won that person back. But if you are unsuccessful, take one or two others with you and go back again, so that everything you say may be*

confirmed by two or three witnesses. If the person still refuses to listen, take your case to the church. Then if he or she won't accept the church's decision, treat that person as a pagan or a corrupt tax collector."

I want to go slowly here because forgiveness is often misunderstood and therefore incorrectly taught. I am not a master at forgiveness, but I can certainly speak from my position of growth through many learning opportunities. The Word teaches that there is a process for forgiving. Process takes time. It takes effort, therefore persistence is implied.

1) *If another believer sins against you, go privately and point out the offense.*

Jesus is instructing Believers on how to deal with other Believers. Ideally, the two disputants will have an equal foundation of belief and practice. If that's the case, it's assumed there's a basic understanding of love, repentance and forgiveness. If not, then at the very minimum, both disputants would know who Jesus is and what His message encourages.

> *process*
> 1. *a systematic series of actions directed to some end*
> 2. *a continuous action, operation, or series of changes taking place in a definite manner*
> 3. *the action of going forward or on*
> (Dictionary.com, 2010)

The message is directed to Believers, however the universal truth of the principle makes the message applicable *in* anyone's life, even a nonbeliever's life. So, for the purpose of your growth, substitute "believer" with "person." *If another person wrongs you, go privately to them and tell them how they hurt you.*

It sounds so simple. But anyone who has lived pass adolescence knows it somehow becomes more difficult with time, increased ego, miscommunication, and any number of other variables. Because of the innumerable complications, I urge you to keep it as simple as possible. In order to do that, you have to know what the true issue is from your perspective. Many people allow offenses to build up before addressing them. They may bring up many situations that caused offense when it's really only one characteristic that's causing an issue (lack of consideration, selfishness, pride, unkind speech, etc.). Before going to the other person, get to the root of the problem with yourself. Know exactly what's troubling you. If it helps, write it down to keep yourself on point. Before you confront, be confident that the confrontation is not only worth the effort but the reason is clear enough to you that you will communicate it to the best of your ability.

Confrontation is a step towards preserving a relationship. Remember that. Work that thought into your words and your actions, because if you didn't care about the relationship, the issue wouldn't matter and you wouldn't waste your time or energy trying to get the other person to see things from your perspective. That's the idea behind confronting and correcting in love. It's working out the kinks in relationships (spousal, parental, family, friend, work, etc.) with a goal of preservation, *not* destruction.

When God confronted Adam in the garden, Adam blamed his actions on his wife, and she blamed the serpent for influencing her.

When you're confronted by a loved one, don't be like Adam and Eve. Mankind stayed in a broken spiritual state for thousands of years before Jesus Christ came to repent and die for Adam's transgression against God. You do not want your human relationships to remain in a fractured or broken state indefinitely.

In *2 Samuel 12:7-10*, God confronted David with the following complaint:

> *I anointed you king of Israel and saved you from the power of Saul. I gave you your master's house and his wives and the kingdoms of Israel and Judah. And if that had not been enough, I would have given you much, much more. Why, then, have you despised the word of the LORD and done this horrible deed? For you have murdered Uriah the Hittite with the sword of the Ammonites and stolen his wife.*

This is awesome to me in several ways, primarily as a direct, itemized complaint. God listed all that He had done in His relationship with David, and all that He was willing to do (David only needed to ask for what he wanted) and finished by asking David how he could act against His Lord in such a way – by murdering a man after he had committed adultery with the man's wife.

There is no possible way David was left wondering what God was upset about.

2) *If the other person listens and confesses it, you have won that person back.*

David listened to God's words through the prophet Nathan and he repented immediately. As clearly wrong as his actions appear to us, he did not see his sin until he was confronted with it. When he repented, God forgave him.

The offender has a truly important, indeed pivotal, role in your forgiveness process. They must acknowledge your complaint. Not only that, they must listen to your complaint and acknowledge their role in damaging the relationship. Their acknowledgement can come in any number of expressions: *I'm sorry; I didn't realize what I did; what can I do to make it up to you?* Your relationship will dictate what's appropriate and acceptable to you.

The offender *must* repent. That's what the confrontation is truly about and what the offended person really wants. They are attempting to establish that the wrong, hurtful behavior will never happen again. However, in order to get that assurance and begin the process of change in the relationship, the offender must first listen and confess their sin (transgression) against the offended party.

The key components of this step are that the offender *listens* to the complaint *and confesses* their offense to the person they injured. After receiving and acknowledging the confession, the injured person can then do their part – offer forgiveness. The scripture say we must forgive as often as an offender confesses their sin and asks our forgiveness *(Matthew 18:21-22)*. The importance of this requirement is discussed in *The Magnitude of Forgiveness*.

3) But if you are unsuccessful, take one or two others with you and go back again, so that everything you say may be confirmed by two or three witnesses.

Sometimes the offender isn't interested in hearing your complaint. Perhaps they aren't too interested in you or the relationship. If they aren't listening, chances are they won't share the reason why. Scripture tells us not to give up on them immediately.

Go back to them with witnesses, ideally neutral peacemakers. Again, the idea is to preserve the relationship. To that end, avoid hurling accusations and ganging up on the offender with biased witnesses.

In the world, the witnesses would be more like mediators to help outline the issue with the offender and help them see not only why the injured person is hurt, but also their desire to mend the relationship. The witnesses could be family members, mutual friends or co-workers or anyone respected by both parties in the conflicted relationship. Whatever the environment your relationship is built in will determine where you look for assistance. The purpose of the witnesses is to verify what is said and done during the confrontation. They should not be used to speak for either party.

Perhaps outside counsel will allow the offender to see beyond their stubbornness. However, if the presence of the witnesses does not work, Jesus tells us to give it yet another try.

4) If the person still refuses to listen, take your case to the church.
At this point the offender is mulishly unrepentant. But even here, we are encouraged to try yet again to win them in love. Believers will take the issue to the church if dealing with another Believer. However, if dealing with a nonbeliever, chances are the complaint will be taken to an authority the nonbeliever recognizes and respects. That could be a matriarch or patriarch of the family, a work supervisor, an independent counselor or perhaps they would agree to speak with the Believer's clergy member.

Again, list your complaint and simply ask them to listen and confess their wrong against you.

5) Then if he or she won't accept the church's decision, treat that person as a pagan or a corrupt tax collector.
At this point, after you have exhausted yourself, your close network and leaders (in other words, you've done all you can do) you are free to back off and leave the unrepentant offender to Jesus.

Chances are, after you have gone through all those channels, no one will be looking favorably on the offender, but you aren't to mistreat them for their stubbornness. The scripture says to treat them as a "pagan or corrupt tax collector." That doesn't sound like good treatment, but Jesus is speaking and He is the messenger of Love. He also told us that whatever we do to the most unworthy people on Earth, we do the same to Him *(Matthew 25:40).*

We've learned that forgiveness without repentance does not restore the relationship. Indeed, restoration isn't possible without repentance first, followed by forgiveness. So what is the proper recourse when the guilty refuse to repent?

Ask the Lord to forgive the offender.

When the relationship ministry (direct confrontation) is ineffective, give the offender and relationship over to God. Ask that He work on the heart of the offender so that the relationship can be restored.

As I write, I am also studying because I want to present the Word as truthfully and as clearly as I am able. My flesh tells me that Step 5 in the process means nothing less than "hold that person in contempt and no longer associate with them" if they refuse to repent (make amends) for the wrong they committed against me. Honestly, that is how I've behaved in the past. However, that is the best reason to doubt this viewpoint – because that is what the flesh wants to do. The flesh is never going to be in line with the spirit and we, as individuals, are responsible for following the desires of the spirit over the desires of the flesh. *Galatians 5:16-18* proclaims:

> *So I say, let the Holy Spirit guide your lives. Then you won't be doing what your sinful nature craves. The sinful nature wants to do evil, which is just the opposite of what the Spirit wants. And the Spirit gives us desires that are the opposite of what the sinful nature desires. These two forces are constantly fighting each other, so you are not free to carry out your good*

intentions. But when you are directed by the Spirit, you are not under obligation to the law of Moses.

Jesus is just as committed to the pagans and tax collectors as He is to God's chosen children. He died for us all. When we hand over the unrepentant offenders in our lives, God's love continues to work on them through the open door of Jesus. There is always hope that a nonbeliever will come to know God's love and seek His forgiveness through interactions with a Believer.

One of the most eye-opening lessons I've learned on my walk with the Lord is that I am unaware of all the offenses *I* have caused. Some people simply stopped talking to me. Others no longer visited. A few walked out of my life, while a couple more withdrew their hospitality. For the most part, I have no idea what caused the drastic shifts in the relationships. I noticed each change and absence and sought the friends out to ask what the issue was. I asked if I had offended. I asked if they wanted to remain friends. I asked if there was anything I could do to help matters. In most cases, I received no answer. In others, I received non-committal replies. I eventually dropped all cases and asked God to forgive any offense I may have caused to anyone unknowingly. I am fine without those relationships. Eventually, I experienced a sense of release from their hold and the desire to pursue them evaporated.

In recognizing my own unintentional culpability with loved ones, I was able to see that offenses towards me may have also been unintentional. Not unintentional in the sense that they were completely unaware of their actions or words, but unintentional in the sense that they may have had no idea how their actions or words would *affect* me. They had no idea how they hurt me. How they crippled me emotionally. How the replay of our damaged relationship shut me down psychologically. They had no idea how they stunted my spiritual growth when they planted their poison into my life.

When I understood that, I understood Jesus's words on the cross on a deeper level,

> *"Father, forgive them, for they don't know what they are doing."*
>
> *~Luke 23:34*

The people who screamed for His death and the guards who nailed Him to the cross were aware of their words and actions. They knew they were participating in physically killing a human being. However, they were clueless as to the ramifications His death would have on the world. I can guarantee you, they didn't think for a second we would be talking about Jesus of Nazareth two thousand years later! To His murderers, His life ended that day. To Believers, His physical death allowed for the revelation of His eternal life upon His resurrection.

Before He physically died, Jesus asked Father God to forgive those tormenting, beating, hating, crippling and murdering Him. Even in the midst of their abuse, as His blood poured from Him on the cross, Jesus expressed His willingness to forgive those trespassing against Him. That's the most profound example of the importance of forgiveness in our lives. It was Jesus's last request during His physical time on Earth.

It's a request repeated by His disciple Stephen as he was stoned to death.

> *As they stoned him, Stephen prayed, "Lord Jesus, receive my spirit." He fell to his knees, shouting, "Lord, don't charge them with this sin!" And with that, he died.*
>
> *~ Acts 7:59-60*

How powerful is the concept that Jesus and Stephen did not want to die without interceding on the behalf of their murderers? They wouldn't be around for the murderers to repent, so they prayed for God the Father not to hold the sin of their murder against the people committing it. Neither left this world without stating their willingness to forgive the final transgression against them.

In *Matthew 18:18* Jesus tells us that whatever we bind on Earth will also be bound in Heaven.

Think about that.

Now, take a moment to consider anything (big or small) you are holding against someone.

I urge you to release whatever is binding you now. Don't wait until you're at the point of death. Don't allow anyone who has requested your forgiveness to go without it. If you have difficulty forgiving a repentant offender, seek God's counsel, ask for His help. His Spirit will take over and assist you in resolving the situation.

It is equally important not to hold any ill feelings towards unrepentant offenders. Ill feelings start off as grudges, hurt and anger and grow to bitterness and resentment. We are admonished to avoid that!

> *Look after each other so that none of you fails to receive the grace of God. Watch out that no poisonous root of bitterness grows up to trouble you, corrupting many.*
> *~ Hebrews 12:15*

Bitterness doesn't only harm you, it poisons others you come in contact with. Your willingness to forgive does your body, mind and spirit good. Practice forgiveness as if your life depends on it. Scratch that. Practice forgiveness as if the lives of your loved ones depend on it, because at some point, it will.

Question: To Forgive or Not to Forgive?

The sacrifices of God are a broken spirit, a broken and a contrite heart — these, O God, You will not despise.
Psalm 51:17

To forgive or not to forgive is a question everyone asks themselves at least once during the course of any given relationship.

The answer is: *forgive*. We are clearly instructed to do so. However, sometimes with forgiveness, *forgiveness* isn't the issue. Perhaps the offenders' nonchalance is the issue. Their lack of care. Their disregard. Sometimes it's the way a person handles the circumstance requiring forgiveness that is the bigger issue. The way they respond or don't respond may cause more hurt and anger than the original offense. The way an offender handles being confronted with their offense speaks to their character and the value they place on the relationship that's in need of righting.

Each party has a role to play in the process of forgiveness. The offended party needs to make the transgression known. The offender needs to:

1. Acknowledge the transgression
2. Address the issue
3. Ask for forgiveness
4. Make restitution

We are instructed to take corrective action when any of our brothers or sisters is injured by us.

> *"So if you are presenting a sacrifice at the altar in the Temple and you suddenly remember that someone has something against you, leave your sacrifice there at the altar. Go and be reconciled to that person. Then come and offer your sacrifice to God."*
>
> *~ Matthew 5:23-24*

Afterwards, if the injured party refuses to forgive, then they have an issue they need to deal with separately. It's important to note that the offender must take responsibility for words or actions that caused harm (direct or indirect; purposeful or not).

Ideally, it would be a wonderful world if we all did exactly what we wanted to do whenever we wanted to do it with no consideration for how other people are impacted by our actions. However, such behavior antagonizes people who encounter it. The attitude associated with it suggests that misbehavior against fellows in Christ should automatically be forgiven. Grace and mercy should instantly be bestowed. This comes from a grievous misunderstanding of Scripture. The people an offender acts against can choose not to take offense or choose to forgive the offense and move on, however the damage done by the offender also harms their own relationship with God.

Unfortunately, that "Christian" attitude is not uncommon. It's also not Christ-like. The nature and principles of Christianity are based on brotherhood, community, and unity. The most common metaphor is that we are members of the same body – the body of Christ. Perhaps it's difficult to recognize and interact with one another because we function in different parts of the body. Perhaps, the left big toe is trying to interact with right ear. They can't see each other too well or grasp each other's function, but that doesn't mean they should treat each other like strangers when their paths cross.

The problem with forcing our "freedom" on others by doing whatever we want with no consideration for our fellow members is that it disrupts the whole *unity* goal. It tarnishes the brotherhood, breaks down the community and certainly gives love a bad name. How can you love someone when you're doing things to them you wouldn't want done to you? How can you call someone brother or sister when your actions repeatedly hurt them? How can you unite with others when you're double-minded?

Jesus said, *"If you love me you will keep my commandments" (John 14:15)* and no commandment is greater than these:

> *"'You shall love the LORD your God with all your heart, with all your soul, and with all your mind.' This is the first and great commandment. And the second is like it: 'You shall love your neighbor as yourself.' On these two commandments hang all the Law and the Prophets."*
>
> *~ Matthew 22:37-39*

Everything that has come before and since falls under the directive of love. Love is the critical piece that works with forgiveness (for the offender and the offended). Love allows patience and provides compassion. Love covers every single sin you can imagine. The whole of God's law is fulfilled when we practice love as instructed.

> *So Christ has truly set us free. Now make sure that you stay free, and don't get tied up again in slavery to the law.*
>
> *For you have been called to live in freedom, my brothers and sisters.* **But don't use your freedom to satisfy your sinful nature.** *Instead, use your freedom to*

> serve one another in love. For the whole law can be summed up in this one command: **"Love your neighbor as yourself." But if you are always biting and devouring one another, watch out! Beware of destroying one another.**
>
> ~ *Galatians 5:1, 13-15, {emphasis mine}*

Wow! The New King James translation of verse 15 says, "If you bite and devour one another, beware lest you be consumed by one another!" That's amazing insight into how our behavior affects not only our walk with God but our fellows in Christ as well.

Our flesh is going to war against other flesh in the body of Christ. That's a major revelation for those looking for peace in the church. Peace is found in the body *only* when the desires of the flesh (pride, envy, back-biting, gossip, control, manipulation, etc.) are denied and the desires of the Holy Spirit (love, joy, peace, self-control, gentleness, etc.) are allowed free reign in your interactions with others.

> *So I say, let the Holy Spirit guide your lives. Then you won't be doing what your sinful nature craves. The sinful nature wants to do evil, which is just the opposite of what the Spirit wants. And the Spirit gives us desires that are the opposite of what the sinful nature desires. These two forces are constantly fighting each other, so you are not free to carry out your good intentions. But when you are directed by the Spirit, you are not under obligation to the law of Moses.*
>
> ~ *Galatians 5:16-18*

True freedom comes when we manifest the fruit of the Spirit in our lives. We are told when the fruit is evident, *then* there is no law against us.

> But the Holy Spirit produces this kind of fruit in our lives: love, joy, peace, patience, kindness, goodness, faithfulness, gentleness, and self-control. **There is no law against these things!**
>
> Those who belong to Christ Jesus have nailed the passions and desires of their sinful nature to His cross and crucified them there. Since we are living by the Spirit, let us follow the Spirit's leading in every part of our lives. Let us not become conceited, or provoke one another, or be jealous of one another.
>
> ~ Galatians 5:22-26, {emphasis mine}

So the true questions are: What is love? What is joy? What are peace, longsuffering, kindness, goodness, faithfulness, gentleness, and self-control?

God is love. Obeying Him brings us joy. Trusting Him gives us peace. Longsuffering is patience; we build and perfect patience through our faithfulness – meaning when we faithfully obey God. Kindness, goodness, and gentleness are a matter of looking after others as God looks after us – shining our light in this world. Ah, and self-control – the big one. In a nutshell, self-control does not mean you do whatever you want to do whenever you want to do it.

> **self-control**
> Control of one's emotions, desires, or actions by one's own will
> (Dictionary.com, 2010)

Self-control is discipline of self. Discipline is a portion of the fruit of the Spirit. That's a whopper, isn't it?

People can forgive you, but their forgiveness does you no good if you don't stop doing or saying the things that harm people in your circles. Forgiveness, in and of itself, does not heal the relationship – it frees the forgiver from the pain of the relationship.

The repentance of the offender leads to healing for the relationship.

When repentance doesn't happen, forgiveness can be offered but it's hollow and ineffective in the long-term, because there'll be no change in the offensive behavior. That's why the absence of a repentant heart is a harbinger of the end of the relationship. When a wrongdoer refuses to repent for their harmful words or actions, they are, in essence, expressing a lack of regard for the injured person and their relationship with them.

In my own life, I am willing to forgive anyone as often as they cause an offense, but I have also learned to forgive from a distance those who continuously repeat the same offenses. I haven't reached the point of rubberizing my heart so it bounces back immediately from bruises and breaks. I have embraced self-preservation to carry me through the painful negotiations of relationship restoration or realignment. I believe I have an obligation to my life and growth in Christ to protect the work God has done in me. As a believer and worker in Christ, I cannot allow the uncommitted and the undisciplined to destroy me. To that end, repeat offenders have to earn my trust again. With my trust come my time, focus and loyalty.

We have been granted a way out – we can hand the unrepentant over to God and walk away from the harmful situation.

Dear Transgressor:

Yes, you can be completely forgiven by our Most Gracious and Merciful Heavenly Father. He has already purchased us at an extraordinary cost and made a way for redemption. When we accept Jesus Christ as our Lord and Savior, all of our sins will then be washed away by His blood. God is appeased with the sacrifice He provided for Himself in Jesus Christ.

His example teaches me that giving and receiving forgiveness is a process that requires commitment and sincerity. Honest effort and sacrifice (stepping out of your comfort zone) is evidence of your desire to make amends. Since we are called to be Christ-like, I must ask, what have you sacrificed to appease those you've offended? Do you even know what you're asking forgiveness for? Have you learned from the situation? If so, how have you changed?

You Forgave. Now What?

> *And you must show mercy to those whose faith is wavering. Rescue others by snatching them from the flames of judgment. Show mercy to still others, but do so with great caution, hating the sins that contaminate their lives.*
> Jude 1:22-23

Let it go. And go about your life. All of God's instructions are for you. Not the offender. Nothing you're told to do will increase the offender spiritually. As a result of your action – your love and forgiveness – they may seek God for themselves (if they haven't already). Or if they already know God, they may seek to grow closer to Him through self-examination. Therefore, their spiritual increase will be the result of *their* relationship with their Creator.

God loves us whether we love Him back or not. He loves us whether we obey Him or not. And yes, He still loves us when we mistreat His other children.

Jesus is our Savior whether He is accepted or not. He is God's self-provided sacrifice whether we acknowledge Him or not. And yes, His blood was still shed for us whether we choose to believe it or not.

The Holy Spirit is our Comforter whether we submit or not. The Spirit of God is our guide whether we follow or not. And yes, the Breath of Life is eternal whether we understand it or not.

These are all givens – love, salvation and comfort.

Forgiveness is not a given. It is not automatic. It's a step in the process of building, maintaining, salvaging and restoring relationships.

> *May God give you more and more mercy, peace, and love.*
>
> *~ Jude 1:2*

Negotiating Forgiveness for a Better Relationship

> *Instead, you have burdened Me with your sins and wearied Me with your faults. "I — yes, I alone — will blot out your sins for My own sake and will never think of them again. Let us review the situation together, and you can present your case to prove your innocence.*
> *Isaiah 43:24-26*

Forgiveness is not a free token; it's an invaluable gift.

Some time ago, I saw an illustration in church. The pastor called a man up from the congregation and told him to ask for the Bible in the pastor's hand. The man asked the pastor for his Bible. The pastor gave the man his Bible. Then the pastor said, "Keep asking for my Bible." The man kept asking for the Bible even as he held it in his own hands. The pastor turned to the congregation and said, "How foolish does he look? He has what he asked for. He received it the first time he asked. Now, what is he going to do with it?"

On paper, forgiveness is rather simple. It's a matter of letting things go. It's about releasing the pain and memory of hurts and infractions against you and no longer resenting the person who caused offense. Forgiveness is about moving on from where you were.

When a willingness to forgive is faced with an unwillingness to repent, the offended person can still go through the process of forgiving by giving the situation to God with the request for Him to forgive the unrepentant person. In releasing the unrepentant to the Lord, the offended person is still responsible for releasing the ill feelings associated with the relationship. In the big picture, being willing to forgive the unrepentant counts as much as the act of forgiving the repentant. Both are based on the condition of the heart – open, giving and eager to express God's love.

Instructions to the "Too-Quick-to-Forgive" Person

> *"Come now, let's settle this," says the LORD. "Though your sins are like scarlet, I will make them as white as snow. Though they are red like crimson, I will make them as white as wool. If you will only obey Me, you will have plenty to eat. But if you turn away and refuse to listen, you will be devoured by the sword of your enemies. I, the LORD, have spoken!"*
>
> *~ Isaiah 1:18-20*

Sometimes our willingness to forgive has us offering forgiveness in haste. How can one tell they've been too hasty in forgiving a loved one? For starters, you know you've offered your forgiveness to quickly when the offender hasn't repented, or you accepted repentance without discussing the harmful behavior with the offender (thereby neglecting to express expectations for future interactions).

From my experiences, the unrepentant offenders remain in the same spot (emotionally and psychologically), waiting for the person they've wronged to return and participate in the same habits that led to the offense. They don't want things to change. Their actions show that they don't consider their offenses to be a big deal because forgiveness is usually given without stipulations. They feel free to be themselves (doing and saying whatever they want no matter the pain cause to others), while reprimanding those who take offense as being intolerant of the offender's personality. I have come to realize that repeat offenders are master manipulators who aren't interested in experiencing the consequences of their actions. In fact, they do their best to avoid consequences altogether.

Receiving forgiveness does not absolve the offender from the consequences for their behavior. Every action has a reaction. Every cause has an effect. Each step is followed by another step.

The consequence of treating someone badly is that the relationship will not be what it was before the ill treatment, even after forgiveness has been given. That doesn't have to be a negative. Success usually comes after many failures. For me, the relationship is either better and stronger than it was before the offense, or nothing. Either way, I keep moving, keep learning and keep growing. My hope is that the other party is moving with me, because I refuse to stagnate my growth for any extended period of time, especially for someone who repeatedly takes advantage of our relationship.

Giving stipulations for a better relationship

> *Kind words are like honey – sweet to the soul and healthy for the body.*
>
> *~ Proverbs 16:24*

I reached a point a couple of years ago where I had to sit back and think about how many people in my life had been comfortable treating me in a cavalier fashion. I took a long, hard look at myself and asked myself tough questions. It wasn't just one, two or three people I received such treatment from – it was through the bulk of my relationships. For starters, what attracted such people to me? And why did they continue to treat me in such a dismissive manner?

My openness and generosity attracted them. And they continued to treat me the way they did because I forgave them when they asked and forgot their transgressions without requiring anything from them. These people didn't make an attempt to express any repentance, not even a sincere/specific apology. Usually, just a simple "I'm sorry." And if I was lucky, a "You know I love you!" In addition to that, none of them attempted to make amends for their hurtful behavior. I've spent the majority of my life giving of myself to others until I become emotionally drained. Then I'm left alone to console and refresh myself.

It wasn't until I confronted myself with this situation, that I realized I rarely asked for anything in my relationships. Or rather, I rarely pushed or insisted on anything. In truth, I did ask for what I wanted, but my requests were rarely honored. When I explored this pattern throughout my relationships, I had to accept responsibility for some of the treatment I've received in my relationships. The bottom line is people treated me the way they did because I allowed it.

Not anymore. Now I'm asking for something in my relationships. I want to be wooed. I want to know you're not just after a comfortable foot stool or a quiet ear. I need to know you're interested in contributing to and sustaining a relationship with me. I need to know I'm not in it alone.

The people God has moved out of my life wouldn't cope well with the woman I am today, if our past interactions are anything to go by. Apparently, I spoiled people with the full force of my personality and affection when they were in my good graces.

Similar to how God spoiled Adam, I went out of my way to accommodate others and ease their burdens. Eventually, I became fed up and withdrew. I had been putting out so much on the front end of the relationships that the other person didn't know how to hold up the back end. Meaning, my effort was driving the relationships. They were around for the ease I provided, not because of any love or respect for me.

Now I take issue with making all the outward effort. I need to see that they have a desire for not just the relationship we have but also for a relationship that improves and grows with time.

I'm also done with setting myself aside. Making my life a priority adds value to any relationship from the other person's point of view. This is not to say everything should be about one person; it's very important that relationships be balanced. To that end, both parties should know their worth and respect the other person as an equally worthy partner in the relationship. Relationships should blend the personalities and lives of the involved parties.

Since coming to these realizations and conclusions, I have started to speak on the issues I am interested in improving, correcting or implementing in my current relationships and ask the other person directly if they are interested in maintaining the relationship.

I am a very simple person; childlike in my simplicity sometimes. I offer sincere, honest affection that's seeking after its own kind. Children don't care who's in a bad mood, who doesn't want to be bothered, who's angry at whom – they are always eager to greet loved ones with a kiss and hug. They're exuberant, cheerful, excited, loving, raucous, uninhibited. Children don't hide their affection. They're overt and shameless. It's easy to respond in like manner to a child. That's how I know that such honesty in adult relationships is possible – because it comes so naturally to the young. An open heart is natural; a closed heart is learned. Relationships are meant to be a mutual pursuit.

When we give and receive freely in our relationships, we open ourselves to a universe of possibilities.

> *"Let the children come to me. Don't stop them! For the Kingdom of God belongs to those who are like these children. I tell you the truth, anyone who doesn't receive the Kingdom of God like a child will never enter it." Then He took the children in His arms and placed His hands on their heads and blessed them.*
> ~ *Mark 10:14-16*

Don't miss this! You have to *receive* the kingdom of God like a little child or you will never enter it! The Kingdom is a state of *heart* we live in here on Earth.

Children don't try to save face. They are not concerned with having the upper hand and never admitting to a wrong. God has gifts for us. Many of His blessings can be found in our relationships. Be open and exuberant about the people in your life, and eventually they will return the favor. If you treat your loved ones as if you can take them or leave them, chances are they'll leave.

Children don't remember wrongs, hurts, or anger. They're quick to love and quick to forgive. The world teaches us differently as we age. We "grow" out of such child-like behavior and "mature" into being suspicious of everyone, not needing anyone, telling "little" lies and omitting whole truths.

> *An honest answer is like a kiss of friendship.*
> ~ *Proverbs 24:26*

Being emotionally honest may sound too simple to be effective when looking back from a heart that's been bruised, scared and broken. In adulthood, our emotional honesty may have ended painfully with us vowing never to open ourselves again, never to reveal the truth of our feelings, to keep our love to ourselves, to get what we can out of others without exposing our need for so much more. If you're hiding, camouflaging, fronting, popping your collar and slapping high-fives to the boys and shouting you-go-girl's to the girls, then you're not being honest about where you are. You're putting on a show. There's no sincerity in your approach. No honor in your presence.

At some point you have to accept responsibility for the damage you made in a relationship. Even if the injured party has already expressed their willingness to forgive you (before you repented), you should still confess your error. Doing so will help eliminate any resistance to interacting with you.

I'm not too proud to say, I need love. Affection goes a long way to improving a person's disposition. Like anyone else, I flower when love is showered on me. A hug and a soft word can bring an end to battles. If a relationship has gotten to a point that I fold up my petals, it's not because I want it that way, it's because I need to be wooed into unfurling. Feed me with love and I will feed you the same in return.

> *How sweet are your words to my taste, sweeter than honey to my mouth!*
>
> *~ Psalm 119:103*

Communication

"Keep on asking, and you will receive what you ask for. Keep on seeking, and you will find. Keep on knocking, and the door will be opened to you. For everyone who asks, receives. Everyone who seeks, finds. And to everyone who knocks, the door will be opened.
You parents — if your children ask for a loaf of bread, do you give them a stone instead? Or if they ask for a fish, do you give them a snake? Of course not! So if you sinful people know how to give good gifts to your children, how much more will your Heavenly Father give good gifts to those who ask Him."
Matthew 7:7-11

The "Ask, Receive, Give" Process Explained

> *Then Jesus told them, "I tell you the truth, if you have faith and don't doubt, you can do things like this and much more. You can even say to this mountain, 'May you be lifted up and thrown into the sea,' and it will happen. You can pray for anything, and if you have faith, you will receive it."*
> *Matthew 21:21-22*

Matthew 7:7-11 is the best explanation of the process involved in asking, receiving and giving I've been exposed to. *Matthew 21:21* follows-up with the faith component. We must believe that what we're asking for will come to fruition.

God tells us that if we ask Him for anything we will receive it. If we are looking for something, we will find it. If we are trying to enter someplace, the door will be opened to us. Everything we want in life is a simple matter of opening our mouths to ask for it; opening our arms to receive it; and opening our hearts to share it. In *Matthew 7* we are told that God knows how to give good gifts to His children. If we trust in this truth and do not doubt Him we may receive all He has for us.

Again, our relationship with God is a model for how our relationships with people should be. God requires communication. Our human relationships are no different.

Communication is vital. Proper communication requires a message to have a sender and receiver, as well as acknowledgment of the message on both ends. It involves the imparting or interchange of thoughts, opinions, or information by speech, writing, or signs. Communication remains incomplete when only one person in a relationship is actively practicing it.

Some societal teachings attempt to lead people to believe that we have to *take* what we want. Taking is not scriptural. The best way to get what you want is to *ask* for it – use your voice. Use your words to communicate your needs.

> *vital*
> 1. *of or pertaining to life*
> 2. *being the seat or source of life*
> 3. *necessary to life;*
> 4. *indispensable; essential*
>   (Dictionary.com, 2010)

Once you ask in faith, be ready to receive. *Receiving* is scriptural. Nothing in life is acquired without first receiving it. You have to be available and open to accept what is given. Your readiness may require preparation, cleansing and/or ridding yourself of things and situations that conflict with what you are asking for. Keep this in mind to assist you in understanding that what you ask for today is not guaranteed to arrive tomorrow, next week or next year. It will come when you're ready, or when it's ready, but most likely, when God is ready. Don't concentrate on its expected arrival; concentrate on *getting ready* to receive your blessing.

When God has blessed you with a gift, He expects you to bless others with it. He created us in His image, made us for His love, filled us with His spirit, and trained us to give as He gives. God desires to bless the world and He will – one person at a time, through each of His children (those who believe and obey Him).

Importance of Communication

> *"Look!" He said. "The people are united, and they all speak the same language. After this, nothing they set out to do will be impossible for them! Come, let's go down and confuse the people with different languages. Then they won't be able to understand each other."*
> *Genesis 11:6-7*

"Tell me what you want! I can't read your mind!" Have those words ever been hurled at you? I can honestly say in nearly all of my relationships – friend, family, work, community – whenever I have had regular interactions with someone, I've told the other person to let me know what they needed or wanted and I would be sure to do what I was able to do. Without fail, that's how I communicate my interest in, availability, and willingness to work with them for a mutually beneficial relationship.

Without fail, I can tell you the best responders have always been the people I work with. Why? Perhaps because there is no expectation of mind-reading.

The people who usually assume I know what they need or want are family and long-term friends. True too, those are the same people I most often act on behalf of before hearing them express their needs. Why? Perhaps because there is knowledge of behaviors, habits, and personality.

When you know certain things about people, you can usually anticipate their needs and desires. However, that is not the same as knowing what they're thinking. There's no way of getting around verbally communicating with the people you interact with.

Have you ever considered that God, who knows everything about everything, especially us – He sees us, hears us, reads our heart, knows our desires, knew us before we knew ourselves – even the all-knowing God requires us to speak and act?

Think about that.

We have to ask Him to move in our lives. We have to respond to Him when he speaks to us. We have to do what He tells us to do when He tells us to do it.

He provides so many instructions in his Word that we know we can't just sit and *think* about obeying Him. We know it's not enough to simply *hope* for a particular outcome. It does no good to only *regret* our actions or *think* loving thoughts. We have to *verbalize* our sorrow when we've wronged someone. We have to *speak* and *show* love to the people we care for.

In *Genesis 11* we learn about the Tower of Babel. This is an excellent story that illustrates the importance of communication. Indeed in verses six and seven, God Himself sums up the magnitude of what clear communication can accomplish,

> *"The people are united, and they all speak the same language. After this, nothing they set out to do will be impossible for them! Come, let's go down and confuse the people with different languages. Then they won't be able to understand each other."*

Do you know that when you and another person understand each another, and you are in agreement with God's word, *anything* you choose to do together will be successful? The Word of God says nothing will be impossible for you. You need to know that.

I get so frustrated when people don't speak, when they don't share their ideas or positions, when they don't contribute to a decision-making conversation. When a person withholds their voice, they are withholding the possibility of reaching agreement with you. And whatever you're working on together will be a struggle at the least, or a failure at the most.

Imagine, a very long time ago, everyone spoke the same language, used the same words, understood each other and accomplished great things. Unfortunately, because their unity was in defiance of God's direct instruction to spread out and fill the earth with their children, God created a situation in which the people preferred to get away from people who made no sense to them. The population separated to form families and tribes based on the languages spoken when God confounded their communication.

How's that for a word? When there is no understanding, there is separation.

Communication provides opportunity for unity and deeper fellowship within a relationship.

Read the passage for yourself.

> At one time all the people of the world spoke the same language and used the same words. As the people migrated to the east, they found a plain in the land of Babylonia and settled there.
>
> They began saying to each other, "Let's make bricks and harden them with fire." (In this region bricks were used instead of stone, and tar was used for mortar.) Then they said, "Come, let's build a great city for ourselves with a tower that reaches into the sky. This will make us famous and keep us from being scattered all over the world."

> But the LORD came down to look at the city and the tower the people were building. "Look!" He said. "The people are united, and they all speak the same language. After this, nothing they set out to do will be impossible for them! Come, let's go down and confuse the people with different languages. Then they won't be able to understand each other."
>
> In that way, the LORD scattered them all over the world, and they stopped building the city. That is why the city was called Babel, because that is where the LORD confused the people with different languages. In this way he scattered them all over the world.
>
> *Genesis 11:1-9*

There are some very important lessons in this passage.

1. God will have His way. You can fall in line and make things easy for yourself or be disobedient and reap consequences that will affect the earth (or your family) for generations to come. To this day, we have just as much difficulty communicating with the person next door as we do with people on the other side of the world. Obey God and save yourself some energy!

2. God has given us so much power that anything we imagine, we can do. If you have doubts about your abilities, reread *Genesis 11:6*. In *Matthew 18:19-20*, Jesus tells us, *If two of you agree here on earth concerning anything you ask, my Father in heaven will do it for you. For where two or three gather together as my followers, I am there among them."* Imagine how difficult communicating and understanding must be if we are only required to

find one or two others to be in agreement with us and God! That difficulty highlights why it's so extremely important!
3. According to the *Dictionary of Biblical Imagery*, sun-dried bricks look hard and permanent but they fall apart quickly in the rain or changing weather. "Bricks often appear in [Biblical] contexts where people are constructing their own proud, temporal plans rather than obeying the eternal God." (Leland Ryken, 1998) In the Babel story, the people were united in disobeying God, building for their own honor rather than God's glory, and creating from their own "materials" instead of from God's materials. When we directly oppose God, our best will be as nothing. We need to build on His word, use His stone and mortar and let go of our own bricks and tar.

Failure to Communicate

His words are as smooth as butter, but in his heart is war. His words are as soothing as lotion, but underneath are daggers!
Psalm 55:21

There are many ways communication can fail between people. There are many instructions on how to speak, listen, and guard your heart and your hearing throughout the Bible. One of the main causes of communication failure is a lack of alignment of the heart and mouth. For example, a person who speaks words contrary to what is in their heart. Or one who agrees to something they are opposed to. Whatever actions follow will be at odds to the original request or need.

Locator questions

When Jesus came to the region of Caesarea Philippi, He asked His disciples, "Who do people say that the Son of Man is?"

"Well," they replied, "some say John the Baptist, some say Elijah, and others say Jeremiah or one of the other prophets."

Then He asked them, "But who do you say I am?"

Simon Peter answered, "You are the Messiah, the Son of the living God."

> *Jesus replied, "You are blessed, Simon son of John, because My Father in heaven has revealed this to you. You did not learn this from any human being.*
> *~ Matthew 16:13-17*

Some questions are intended to locate you in your relationship. When God or Jesus asks you a question they want to make you aware of where you are spiritually. When your spouse asks certain questions, chances are they want to know where you are emotionally. When your employer asks you questions, they want to know where you are developmentally. Every relationship will have questions, for which the answers you provide will reveal where you are in that relationship. Your response will tell the requestor if your heart is in it, if you've given serious thought to the situation, and if you've grown since the relationship began. They aren't trick questions; don't be afraid to answer honestly. In fact, the more honest you are, the more you benefit the relationship.

When Jesus asked His disciples who the world thought He was, He received various answers. So, He got more specific, *"Who do you say I am?"*

Keep in mind, Jesus could read the hearts of anyone and often told people what they were thinking before they spoke. He knew what his disciples' thoughts were about Him. He wasn't seeking an answer for Himself. He was seeking to make them aware of where they were in their relationship with their God.

When Simon Peter answered, *"You are the Messiah, the Son of the living God,"* and Jesus replied, *"My Father in Heaven revealed this to you, because no human being taught you this,"* Peter learned he had a direct spiritual connection to the Father. He was in communication with the Holy Spirit. Up to that point, Peter was most likely unaware of where he was in his walk with God. His answer to Jesus's question revealed his spiritual growth and development.

In communication, it's important to not make assumptions. Never assume your words are understood and agreed with as you spoke them. You may think your speech is clear, but your message may not have been heard. You may think your delivery was impeccable but it may not have been well received. Ask follow-up questions. Ask your listeners what they heard. Not in a condescending way, but to see if you hear back what you intended to convey.

Likewise, if you're receiving communication, ask follow-up questions rephrased in words you're more familiar with. For example, cross-generational communication would benefit from rephrasing and repeating requests. Over the course of the last century, "calling" someone has changed from visiting them at home, telephoning them at home, telephoning them on their mobile phone to texting to video-phoning them on their mobile phone or computer. Depending on when the bulk of your socializing took place during the last century, you would be more familiar making one type of call.

If you must make an assumption in communication, assume that your audiences' frame of reference is different from yours – even if you've known them for a long time.

Daily life has a way of altering our perspective, preferences and responses. Something that made sense last year for a project may seem completely off base this year because you've been exposed to additional options. Communicating with someone whose opinion or viewpoint hasn't changed may be difficult and lead to tension.

In *My God and Me: Listening, Learning and Growing on My Journey*, I wrote about an adulterous proposition I received from a married man. I asked him if his wife knew he was on the phone propositioning me. (Jones, 2009) During one of my book discussions, a woman mentioned this exchange with a laugh, "You ask some stupid questions in this book!" Others laughed along. I replied, "The questions do sound simple." I should've added, *"If you assume you know the answer."*

I had met that man at the same time I met his wife and had received career encouragement from them both. I thought it was rather cavalier and disrespectful for him to even think what he was thinking. The only answer I gave to his proposition was my question about his wife. He never called me again.

It may sound like a stupid question to some, but I thought it was rather direct. It was a question intended to remind him of his status. He wasn't his to give – he no longer belonged to himself. Any decision he made regarding his life and body affected someone else – his wife. The fact that he was on the phone with me trying to get something started told me he wasn't thinking about his obligations and commitment to his wife.

In the end, we both understood one another. But the fact that we had communicated enough, and to a degree that he felt comfortable proposing a sinful relationship to me revealed we both failed at communication early on. We both saw and heard something other than what was intended. He didn't understand I was only interested in employment assistance and I didn't understand he was only interested in helping for a price.

An opportunity to correct yourself

> *When the cool evening breezes were blowing, the man and his wife heard the LORD God walking about in the garden. So they hid from the LORD God among the trees. Then the LORD God called to the man, "Where are you?"*
>
> ~ Genesis 3:8-9

One of the most profound questions in the Bible is, *"Where are you?" (Genesis 3:9)* God asked this of Adam after he ate the fruit. Does anyone really believe God didn't know where Adam was? Adam's physical location was not the purpose of the question. Adam's disobedience separated him from God spiritually. Their fellowship was broken. The question served two purposes: to illustrate the broken relationship and to make Adam aware of his sin.

God went searching for Adam to give him the opportunity to acknowledge his sin, accept responsibility, repent (make amends) for his disobedience and mend the spiritual breach. God confronted Adam with his sin because He wanted to forgive him. He wanted to squash the issue then and there. Put it to rest, sort of speak. But he couldn't forget about it until it was forgiven. And He couldn't forgive the sin until the offender repented.

Did you get all of that from *"Where are you?"* With that question, God was also saying, "I'm here. I'm looking for you. I want you. Come back to me!"

Adam, that spoiled, pampered man for whom God had provided everything – even his woman (he went to sleep alone one night and woke up the next morning with Eve tucked into his side) – yes, that Adam never had to do anything. Apparently, he didn't trouble himself with thinking things through either. He basically told God, his creator, "Look, this separation is your fault. You gave me this headstrong woman who took it upon herself to listen to that wily snake. She chose to hand-feed me the fruit you told me not to eat. If she hadn't put it in my mouth, I wouldn't have eaten it. Really, what did you expect of me?"

Adam's response revealed where he was in his relationship with his God. His heart was far from God. He felt no obligation to God over and above what he and his wife wanted to do.

Whenever there's the command to love God in the Bible, it is followed by a description of how to show that love – primarily by obeying His commands and instructions. We obey God by keeping his words in us – in our heart and mouth.

Eve knew what God's instructions were. We know this because she repeated them back to the serpent. But neither she nor Adam had placed those words in their hearts. The fact that they chose to listen to one of God's created creatures over God Himself exhibited the value they placed on God and their relationship with Him.

"Adam, where are you?" comes across as a gut-wrenching parental cry at the loss of child. Adam and Eve had rejected God – His spirit, love and life – with that single, seemingly simple decision. They had the choice of life and death and eagerly chose death, even as they sat in the midst of paradise. They could see what *life* looked like, felt like, sounded and smelled like. They already knew what life *tasted* like! They had the option of having all that every day for eternity. But they thought they were missing out on something and chose to go with Fruit Tree #2.

I'm certain God thought His communication to Adam was clear and emphatic. I'm sure He considered the communication fair. He is the Creator, after all. He spoke to His creation about aspects of the environment He had provided for him. He ensured the message was sent and received.

My heart tells me that God had hoped that Adam would choose Him. Yes, He had given Adam free will – the opportunity to choose as he wanted – but He had stacked the deck in His own favor. Adam had a perfect life – no knowledge of beginning or ending; one day, he just was. He had work to do with his hands and mandatory rest periods to enjoy time with his Lord. Everywhere he looked, he saw beauty. Food was provided in abundance. And a companion was created specifically for him. God had done so much for Adam, there should have been no contest between the known and the unknown.

Even God didn't assume the outcome of a communication in an environment nearly free of distractions. Of course, He had a preferred outcome and the scales had been tipped in His favor, but as illustrated, in *Genesis 3*, it only takes *one* distraction, one changed word or a juxtaposition of a phrase to alter follow-through, results, understanding, relationship and fellowship.

Communication is the responsibility of both the speaker and listener. We have a responsibility to speak what's in our hearts and hear what is being said. Once heard, the response should be in accordance to what was originally said. Whether you agree or disagree, you need to verbalize your understanding and position. Let the other person know where you are so you can both work on moving closer together in your relationship and closer to God.

Self-Communication

You will grieve, but your grief will suddenly turn to wonderful joy. It will be like a woman suffering the pains of labor. When her child is born, her anguish gives way to joy because she has brought a new baby into the world. So you have sorrow now, but I will see you again; then you will rejoice, and no one can rob you of that joy. At that time you won't need to ask Me for anything. I tell you the truth, you will ask the Father directly, and He will grant your request because you use My name. You haven't done this before. Ask, using My name, and you will receive, and you will have abundant joy.
John 16:20-24

On January 29, 2010, I updated my Facebook status to the following:

LaShawnda Jones is refreshed, renewed and restored!

2010 is not the year I beg people to stay in my life. Said with a deep abiding love for them and for me. If you're not even trying to love and respect me with the love God commanded all His people to have for one another – keep it moving! You're blocking my blessings; I need to make room to receive all God wants to give me. Do your best to be true to you and I'll continue to be true to me. God bless.

That was such a powerful statement for me that I chronicled it in my journal immediately after posting. I had come to a point in my life that *love* had become uncompromising. Up to that point of my journey, I thought that my love for others would allow me to withstand their abuse and neglect of me indefinitely. Not true. Love needs to be loved. Love needs to be protected. Since the people I loved weren't caring for me, I had to step away and care for myself, otherwise, I was at risk of being destroyed.

The remainder of my journal entry stated:

> *I'm done with the dead relationships; the stagnant albatrosses that refuse to move or grow. I'm done with people who are just holding a spot in my life but not contributing anything for the space and time they're taking from me. I'm done looking to people to be true representatives of You, Father. From now on I will endeavor to move in relationships only when I clearly hear your mark and receive your confirmation. I desire to kill my flesh, Father, and all its earthly/worldly desires. I want to grow more in You with a prospering body, mind, and spirit. In the matchless, marvelous name of Jesus and by Your most gracious and enduring Spirit, Father, I pray this and more – please search my heart. Amen!*

Do you know what messages you're internalizing? Do you know which messages you're holding on to and regurgitating? What you believe and what you say should be seamless. Our God is a God of compassion; He has everlasting patience; and He has already made forgiveness available whenever anyone is ready to ask for it. But none of that means He wants any of His children – His chosen, those who believe in Him – to endanger themselves and their relationship with Him by keeping themselves in situations or relationships that continually harm them and chip away at their faith. Yes, our faith will be tested and we are instructed to withstand those tests, but in all your getting, get understanding *(Proverbs 4:7)* – test the spirits testing you *(1 John 4:1)*! In this way, you will learn the difference between people and situations intent on strengthening you through your trials and those intent on destroying you from your spirit outward.

Encourage yourself in the Lord *(1 Samuel 30:6)*! Build yourself up in His Kingdom by feeding on His Word. Look to God for examples and outlines on how to live and love, receive and give. When you take your lead from God, He will temper and strengthen you. Your words may come out sounding extremely soft to some and unnecessarily harsh to others, but they will be just right for you.

Pop Culture

vs.

The Bible

So do not corrupt yourselves by making an idol in any form — whether of a man or a woman, an animal on the ground, a bird in the sky, a small animal that scurries along the ground, or a fish in the deepest sea. And when you look up into the sky and see the sun, moon, and stars — all the forces of heaven — don't be seduced into worshiping them. The LORD your God gave them to all the peoples of the earth. Remember that the LORD rescued you from the iron-smelting furnace of Egypt in order to make you His very own people and his special possession, which is what you are today.

Deuteronomy 4:16-20

Led Astray by Pop Culture

> *But I am afraid that as the serpent deceived Eve by his cunning, your thoughts will be led astray from a sincere and pure devotion to Christ.*
> 2 Corinthians 11:3

The world is a morass of miscommunication. Values are backwards. Elements associated with acceptable social status are skewed. American culture is envied by people all around the world, but as a Believer living in the center of the modern American Babylon, New York City, I'd argue that some third world countries may be closer to practicing God's truth than Americans are as a nation.

A country that was birthed on the ideals of freedom, justice, brotherhood and unity (not coincidentally, Biblical principles for a life well-lived) has degraded itself to a degree that sex, lies, cruelty and death are the main attractions in entertainment and society. It's disgusting. It's frightening. It's painful.

One of my favorite movie lines was spoken in the midst of a movie representing the best and the worst of society. The line was barked in outrage on the witness stand of a courtroom by Jack Nicholson's Marine character, Colonel Jessep, in *A Few Good Men*. Tom Cruise's character, Lieutenant Kaffee, was grilling the Colonel for the truth of his involvement in the death of a soldier under his command.

> "You want answers," Colonel Jessup snapped.
> "I want the truth," Lieutenant Kaffee demanded.
> "You can't handle the truth!"
>
> (Reiner, 1992)

What a powerful statement. A rare truth in pop culture.

I look at the way we have devolved as a nation, a society, a culture – as a people – and I see generations of people who can't handle the truth. They don't recognize the truth of who they are. They can't comprehend the truth of their purpose in this world. They embrace lies based on images and idolatry. Indeed, some of the devil's favorite playgrounds must be the American entertainment businesses – television, cinema, music, sports and social media. Anything where people have "followers" and "fans" that make them feel as if they are more than they truly are, or where the "followers" and "fans" feel less than who they truly are themselves.

> *Because of the privilege and authority God has given me, I give each of you this warning: Don't think you are better than you really are. Be honest in your evaluation of yourselves, measuring yourselves by the faith God has given us. Just as our bodies have many parts and each part has a special function, so it is with Christ's body. We are many parts of one body, and we all belong to each other.*
>
> *Romans 12:3-5*

People who are lifted onto pedestals eventually believe in their "superstar" persona. They believe they are above the masses. They buy into their false deity status. In such a state of delusion, the "stars" neglect to properly, effectively and honestly evaluate themselves. They lose sight of themselves as a created being and begin to think of themselves as self-created assets. They measure themselves against other people or material consumption. People who are completely tuned to outward matters – appearance, admiration, wealth, status, etc. – are completely out of touch with inward matters – faith, spiritual growth and walking in love. They present themselves as idols and set themselves up to be worshipped, indeed, the adulation is what they earnestly seek.

The "followers" and "fans" of such people are no better. The Biblical term for them is "idolater." Merely liking someone and enjoying their work isn't idolatry. However, excessive admiration of anyone or anything is idolatry.

Though I reference the entertainment industries, the "superstar-minded" can be found in any setting – home, community, school, office, the military....

In *A Few Good Men*, after stunning the fictitious courtroom and mesmerized viewers, Colonel Jessep continued with the most scathing *I-am-God-and-you-aren't-worth-my-breath* tirade I have ever heard in life or fiction.

> *Son, we live in a world that has walls and those walls have to be guarded by men with guns. Who's gonna do it? You? I have a greater responsibility than you can possibly fathom. You weep for Santiago [dead Marine the trial is for] and curse the Marines. You have that luxury. You have the luxury of not knowing what I know. Santiago's death, while tragic, probably saved lives. And my existence, while grotesque and incomprehensible to you, saves lives! You don't want the truth, because deep*

down, in places you don't talk about at parties, you want me on that wall. You need me on that wall!

We use words like honor, code, loyalty. We use these words as the backbone of a life spent defending something! You use them as a punch line!

I have neither the time nor inclination to explain myself to a man who rises and sleeps under the blanket of the very freedom that I provide and then questions the manner in which I provide it! I would rather that you just said, "Thank you" and went on your way. Otherwise, I suggest you pick up a weapon and stand at post. Either way, I don't give a damn what you think you are entitled to!

(Reiner, 1992)

If there were compassion or love in that speech, rather than disdain and contempt, I could imagine God speaking those words to any one of His creation. But the words weren't spoken by God or a character representing God. They were spoken by a character who imagined He had god-like powers – the choice of life and death over anyone within his realm. Colonel Jessep is a character based on someone and reminiscent of someone else. His most egregious sin is thinking he is more than he is.

Be careful you don't do the same.

Influence of Culture

> *Don't copy the behavior and customs of this world, but let God transform you into a new person by changing the way you think. Then you will learn to know God's will for you, which is good and pleasing and perfect.*
> *~ Romans 12:2*

People are as likely to develop their values and beliefs from movies, songs, fashion or political rhetoric. America has become a society of idol worshipers with no understanding of the grievous sin committed repeatedly throughout any given day. You need to know that ignorance of God's laws does not exonerate you from the consequences of disobedience.

The Bible warns us about how the ways of the world and the leanings of the flesh are contrary to the desires of the Holy Spirit.

A summary of how the world views love and forgiveness is simply, "Say whatever you need to say to get what you want." The first lie we learn in society is: words don't matter. When a person accepts that lie as a truth they begin speaking words they don't mean. They make promises they don't intend to keep. Or they keep silent and mislead you with their suggestive motions. From there, any lie can reap significant damage and the truth loses value.

Be careful! Check your cultural influences! Retreat from everything that hurt s your faith walk. Followers of Christ live in the world, but are not *of* the world. They live according to faith, not environment. Circumstances should not dictate how Believers represent Jesus Christ, our Lord and Savior. Nor should circumstances prevent true Believers from earnestly seeking God first always.

> *... a true Jew is one whose heart is right with God. And true circumcision is not merely obeying the letter of the law; rather, it is a change of heart produced by God's*

Spirit. And a person with a changed heart seeks praise from God, not from people.

~ Romans 2:29

Oneness of Giving & Receiving

"Do not judge, and you will not be judged. Do not condemn, and you will not be condemned. Forgive, and you will be forgiven. Give, and it will be given to you. A good measure, pressed down, shaken together and running over, will be poured into your lap. For with the measure you use, it will be measured to you."
Luke 6:37-38

"Who has ever given to God, that God should repay them?" For from Him and through Him and for Him are all things. To Him be the glory forever! Amen.
Romans 11:35-36

Oneness

In the beginning the Word already existed. The Word was with God, and the Word was God. He existed in the beginning with God. God created everything through Him, and nothing was created except through Him. The Word gave life to everything that was created, and His life brought light to everyone. The light shines in the darkness, and the darkness can never extinguish it.
John 1:1-5

All of God's creation is one – one source, one spirit, one love, and one light. Apart from God, nothing exists (Romans 11:36). We exist only through Him. His hands formed our bodies from dust. His spirit animates our bodies. His breath gives life to our soul. Because we are all one with the Creator of the universe – all that is seen and unseen – we are also one with all of creation. We are one with each other.

When God gave us life, He didn't lose life. When He gave us His spirit, His Holy Spirit did not diminish. Likewise when He fills us with love, He is not depleted of love. Nor is His light dimmed when we decide to walk into it.

Throughout the whole of the scriptures, God petitions man to partake of all He is by seeking Him, accepting Him, praising Him and feeding on His Word. When we depend on the Lord, He abundantly provides for all our needs, allowing for joy to become a way of life.

Ask and you will receive, and your joy will be complete.
~ John 16:24

Hearty Matters

The heart is the passage through which we give to, and receive from, others. We must open our hearts in order to distribute and process all our blessings.

What changes do you want to see in your life and in your relationships? In the timeless words of Mahatma Gandhi, "you must be the change you wish to see in the world." Your improved relationships begin with *you*.

> *One person gives freely, yet gains even more; another withholds unduly, but comes to poverty. A generous person will prosper; whoever refreshes others will be refreshed.*
> *~ Proverbs 11:24-25 NIV*

The most common phrases I've heard in life are about the Biblical principle of giving and receiving – *you reap what you sow; you harvest what you plant; you get back what you put out;* and *karma*. When people talk about karma or one's actions returning a like reward, they're talking about giving and receiving. Your actions set off a chain of reactions that eventually work back around to you.

There is no separation between giving and receiving. Both giving and receiving requires reciprocity. It's a principle that works.

The condition of the heart of both the giver and the receiver matters in regard to any exchange. What was intended? What was felt – appreciation, love, gratitude, consideration? Giving is a loving gesture. So is receiving.

give	receive
to present voluntarily and without expecting compensation	to take into one's possession (something offered or delivered)
to relinquish or sacrifice	to hold, bear, or contain
to place in someone's care	to accept from another (also by hearing or listening)
to convey or transmit; to be connected with	to take into the mind; apprehend mentally

(Dictionary.com, 2010)

A generous person will be rewarded generously. Likewise, a miserly person will be treated with miserliness. Whatever condition your heart is in when you give and receive will determine how you are rewarded for your actions. For example, if you give an extravagant gift with a heart full of resentment, anger, jealously or pride, then the gift is coming from the heart of a miser. On the flip side, you can pick a flower on the side of the road and give it to a friend because something about that flower brought them fondly to mind. That is a gift that comes from a generous heart – a heart full of love and consideration for another.

> *Know the state of your flocks, and put your heart into caring for your herds, for riches don't last forever, and the crown might not be passed to the next generation.*
> *~ Proverbs 27:23*

The Difference Between Believers & Nonbelievers

But if we are living in the light, as God is in the light, then we have fellowship with each other, and the blood of Jesus, His Son, cleanses us from all sin.
If we claim we have no sin, we are only fooling ourselves and not living in the truth. But if we confess our sins to Him, He is faithful and just to forgive us our sins and to cleanse us from all wickedness. If we claim we have not sinned, we are calling God a liar and showing that His word has no place in our hearts.
1 John 1:7-10

In 2010 I separated from the first church congregation I had joined and actively participated in. It had been a tumultuous, confusing and painful three years of membership. I didn't really feel as if I shared true fellowship with anyone in the congregation. All my attempts to connect had been scorned, ignored or exploited. The only thing that kept me from thinking it was all my fault was my ability to see God working in my life, even in the midst of my church turmoil.

During my last month at that church, I came across a book by Philip Gulley titled, *If the Church Were Christian*. The title identified the greatest weight on my heart regarding the "church" I was leaving. Perhaps it would better and more accurate to identify that group as "the congregation" I was leaving. The majority of the people I interacted with in the congregation were not Christian to me. I didn't see Christ reflected in their faces or their actions. Perhaps I was looking too hard or maybe it wasn't for me to see Christ in them. They used words to claim their hearts belonged to God, but I walked away from gatherings feeling tainted. The way some of them treated me and others gave a lie to what they professed to believe.

I've been accused of being a perfectionist. I've received complaints that my expectations of people are too high. Recently, I've been admonished that "people are people" in response to my critique of the congregation I separated from. Someone in both my former and current churches spoke the words, "people are people" to explain the un-Christian behavior of the church members. Perhaps not intentionally, their caution appeared to have the goal of bringing my high-mindedness back down to the gritty reality of earthly living. The translation to me was that I shouldn't expect anymore from Christians than I would from non-Christians. They were telling me that Believers commit sins and offend people just like non-believers. Believers lie, cheat and manipulate just like any other person. That's what I heard when the two Christian women, generations apart and from two separate congregations reprimanded me for my expectation to see God reflected in the lives and behaviors of the congregation I fellowship with.

I've been mulling that over for some time now. My response to the "people are people" theorists is: Believers are called out of the masses! God has a chosen people that are not *of* this world! God's people are not deceivers, manipulators, adulterers, harlots, thieves or destroyers. Believers may have histories that reflect such behavior but when they *surrender all* to God and *accept Him fully* into their heart, He washes all that they *were* away. He cleanses them. He renews them and continually makes them into a new creation through the renewing of their hearts and minds.

> *My dear children, I am writing this to you so that you will not sin. But if anyone does sin, we have an advocate who pleads our case before the Father. He is Jesus Christ, the one who is truly righteous. He himself is the sacrifice that atones for our sins — and not only our sins but the sins of all the world.*
>
> *~ 1 John 2:1-2*

I strenuously resist the disastrous thought that God's Church, the true body of Christ, is made up of people who are content to behave as people of the world behave. I reject the notion that I should accept and associate with people who claim to be followers of Christ yet they never reflect Him. Scripture is very clear on how anyone can identify followers of Christ (Believers): *The world will know you by your love for one another!* So why have I not experienced love in my congregation? Why have I not felt secure, hopeful and at peace among my fellows in Christ?

> *And we can be sure that we know Him if we obey His commandments. If someone claims, "I know God," but doesn't obey God's commandments, that person is a liar and is not living in the truth. But those who obey God's word truly show how completely they love Him. That is how we know we are living in Him. Those who say they live in God should live their lives as Jesus did.*
>
> *~ 1 John 2:3-6*

If I walk into a church with an open heart full of love, but leave the church with an empty heart closed up from bruising attacks and disillusionment, then I've concluded that I'm not walking away from God's people – I'm not leaving *His* church – I'm walking away from people in the world camouflaging themselves as Christians.

There is a life preserving difference between a Believer and a non-believer.

You can't just say you're a Christian and expect to be worthy of fellowship with Believers. You can't just parrot scripture and hope to be saved by the blood of Jesus. God's Word is alive and active when it's simply in the air. But, when His Word is *in* His people – WOW, watch out! – His power is visible. His presence is unmistakable, and His love touches lives beyond the body He inhabits.

A person's heart and life are not mutually exclusive. When you truly believe God exists and He sacrificed His firstborn Son for the lives of all who come after Him – then the power of that belief transforms your life. That person may tell a lie, but they will come back and correct themselves. You may walk a wrong path for a time, but you will retrace your steps to get back on the right path. Your may struggle with selfishness, but you will be convicted through random opportunities to act selflessly.

> *So we have stopped evaluating others from a human point of view. At one time we thought of Christ merely from a human point of view. How differently we know Him now! This means that anyone who belongs to Christ has become a new person. The old life is gone; a new life has begun!*
>
> *2 Corinthians 5:16-17*

I don't believe in a perfect world nor do I believe in perfect people. However, I do believe in a perfect, all-seeing God who works through our lives to perfect our hearts, minds, and spirits. His tool of perfection is His love. When His people use His love in their lives to plant it in other people's lives, we become living testimonies and witnesses of the power of love to transform the world, one life at a time.

The difference is conviction. You can't love God with all your heart, mind, soul and strength, then mistreat His people. He deposited Himself into all of His creation. Jesus Christ says whatever anyone does to the least of mankind, they do to Him. Likewise, whatever anyone does to the best of mankind, they do to Jesus also. When people mistreat people, they mistreat God. When a Believer mistreats people, they are a traitor to the Word and their acts of treason are against the Kingdom of Heaven and the Lord of All.

Acceptance is Crucial

*Therefore, accept each other just as Christ has
accepted you so that God will be given glory.
I bring you the Good News so that I might present
you as an acceptable offering to God, made holy by the
Holy Spirit.
Romans 15:7, 16*

I feel as if I've written a thesis paper. I hope and pray my outline and defense of the Heavenly principles of love, repentance and forgiveness benefits the Kingdom and cause no harm. Trying to decide how to conclude this volume led to several false starts.

God is good and His grace abounds always! Hallelujah! My patience is not perfect, but I have learned to sit and wait on the Lord! AMEN!

As in all things, He directed me on how to close this volume.

There is a common thread uniting love, repentance and forgiveness. What takes place when someone makes the effort to ask for love, repentance or forgiveness? What has happened when someone is courageous enough to open themselves to receiving love, repentance and forgiveness? What is the significance of giving love, repentance and forgiveness?

Each situation requires the asker, receiver, and giver to open themselves. Expose themselves. Make themselves vulnerable. In their vulnerability, they are giving the best of themselves – the true essence of their spirit.

Giving of yourself is a God-centered, Word-inspired selfless act. We can choose to give the best of who we are every day in every relationship.

Before anyone can effectively give of themselves, they must first accept who they are. Once self-acceptance has taken place, one will be open to accepting all that God is. Or more exactly: When one accepts God into their heart, they then have the ability to see themselves as they truly are. At that point, they can bless themselves with self-forgiveness and accept everything that they are, as-is. Either way, both God-acceptance and self-acceptance are necessary before one is able to accept another person. Please note, accepting a person as they are is not the same as tolerating someone because you "care" about them.

> *accept*
> 1. *to take or receive (something offered); receive with approval or favor*
> 2. *to undertake the responsibility, duties, honors, etc., of*
> 3. *to accommodate or reconcile oneself to*
> 4. *to receive without adverse reaction*
> (Dictionary.com, 2010)

Many people hate themselves, but think they are capable of loving others with the same heart. That's not possible. Remember: God is love. The love we are suppose to spread in the world is of God, whether we recognize it or not. Love does not coexist with hate.

> *God is love, and all who live in love live in God, and God lives in them. And as we live in God, our love grows more perfect. So we will not be afraid on the day of judgment, but we can face him with confidence because we live like Jesus here in this world.*

> *Such love has no fear, because perfect love expels all fear.*
>
> *~ 1 John 4:16-18*

The Bible uses the word "fear;" hate is a form of fear – fear of truth, perfection, completion. Fear of salvation, love and acceptance. If you hate anyone (yourself, God, others) you're basically scared of something. It's really that simple.

You're either scared of who you were, who you are, or who you're becoming. Perhaps you're terrified of all three tenses of yourself. If you hate another person, most likely, you hate what's reflected back to you of yourself from interactions with them. Fear and its derivatives can be explored in another *MeatyWord* volume, however, the important thing to remember here is that, in the most extreme cases, *Fear & Co.* move love out of the heart; and in the least, they overshadow any love that may be in the heart. Therefore, whether you hate yourself or others, you're not capable of loving anyone (especially not God) with the same heart.

> *If someone says, "I love God," but hates a Christian brother or sister, that person is a liar; for if we don't love people we can see, how can we love God, whom we cannot see? And he has given us this command: Those who love God must also love their Christian brothers and sisters.*
>
> *~ 1 John 4:20-21*

One of the most amazing revelations about God's creative genius with His masterpiece, mankind (men and women), is that "creation" is an evolutionary process on every level, but most spectacularly on an individual level.

Here's an elementary example of God's evolutionary process. Two fully developed humans (man and woman) come together to produce from seeds they were both born with. The female contributes her egg, XX, and the male contributes his fertilizing seed, XY. The combined contribution produces a baby (male or female) that enters the world through the woman's womb. That's the physical birth; the first birth. The baby grows into a child then an adult.

> *evolution*
> 1. *any process of formation or growth; development*
> 2. *a process of gradual, peaceful, progressive change or development*
> 3. *a motion incomplete in itself, but combining with coordinated motions to produce a single action*
> (Dictionary.com, 2010)

During the physical evolutionary process, the child or adult eventually uncovers the spiritual seed planted in them before their birth and begin to feed, nurture, and develop it. At some point in the process of cultivating their spiritual seed and the fruit produced from it, they encounter the truth of Jesus Christ the Messiah. Upon the point of accepting everything Jesus is and the totality of His work done on behalf of mankind, (specifically for each individual's benefit), the person enters the Kingdom of God. This is a spiritual birth; the second birth.

> *Jesus told him, "I am the way, the truth, and the life. No one can come to the Father except through Me. If you had really known Me, you would know who My Father is. From now on, you do know Him and have seen Him!"*
>
> *~John 14:6-7*

We are spirits housed in bodies living in this world. As such, we are susceptible to the by-product of this world: decay, corruption and destruction. We are target-practice for the enemy of God (*a.k.a.* Satan, the devil) whose primary goal is to steal, kill and destroy us *(John 10:10)*, our inheritance and most especially our *relationship* with God our Father. Because we are constantly in the line of fire, we must constantly re-enforce our defenses. Faith is our shield; the Word of God is our sword *(Ephesians 6:16-17)*. God Himself renews our heart, mind and spirit to keep us in *or* return us to right standing with Him.

> *Create in me a clean heart, O God. Renew a loyal spirit within me. Do not banish me from your presence, and don't take your Holy Spirit from me. Restore to me the joy of your salvation, and make me willing to obey you.*
> ~ *Psalm 51:10-12*

This has been an elaborate tour around worldly and heavenly instances to make a solid argument for my point: *a person must first accept themselves as they are and God as He is, in order to fully give of themself and receive from others.* It's God's job to make us into the person He wants us to be, and believe Him, He will do it!

> *For God in all His fullness was pleased to live in Christ, and through Him God reconciled everything to Himself. He made peace with everything in Heaven and on Earth by means of Christ's blood on the cross.*
>
> *This includes you who were once far away from God. You were His enemies, separated from Him by your evil thoughts and actions. Yet now He has reconciled you to Himself through the death of Christ in His physical body. As a result, He has brought you into His own presence, and you are holy and blameless as you stand before Him without a single fault.*
> ~ *Colossians 1:19-22*

Duality of Man: Strength and Vulnerability

And he will stand to lead his flock with the LORD's strength, in the majesty (power) of the name of the LORD his God. Then his people will live there undisturbed (securely), for he will be highly honored around the world.
Micah 5:4

How does one write a finale to a book that begins with love and forgiveness and centers on repentance? This book should have gone to my editor in November 2010, but it wasn't even done. In fact, the whole month of November went by without me writing one substantive word for the final two chapters. The timing is significant because I was scheduled to publish in January 2011, and had already booked media to promote the completed book.

Dream of a Vision

The week of Thanksgiving brought several personal revelations to me through the resurfacing of a dormant family relationship. Following those revelations, I had a series of dreams that added dimensions to the message.

The most vivid dream in the series involved a man (not a relative). In each scene the man appeared in, he was standing tall with firmly planted feet and a broad welcoming smile. Perched on his left hip, like an attachment, was a big baby boy who looked to be three or four years old. He was a beautiful boy with bright alert eyes – piercing, really – and a much older mischievous expression. Physically, the toddler didn't resemble the man at all, yet there was an element of sameness and familiarity.

The man greeted me and indicated in the conversation that the toddler was one and a half years old. I commented that the baby boy was more than twice the size of the average toddler his age. Even as I said that, I was reaching over to hug and kiss the baby boy. The man's countenance glowed with illuminating joy when I stepped back to face him. He then embraced me. End dream sequence.

Upon waking, I was confused about elements of the dream. Primarily, who was the big baby/toddler boy? As I mentally walked back through the dream, I discarded the idea of the boy being the man's son or other relative, and concluded the big baby was the man himself, representing a part of the man that was less mature, even though he looked over-developed. The baby/toddler seemed to represent a part of the man that was extremely vulnerable, even though he appeared to ooze mischief, knowledge and awareness.

Accept all of me...
What was it about the dream that inspired a retelling?

The man presented his vulnerabilities to me and I embraced them (symbolized by kissing and hugging the baby). The joy the man received from that acceptance lead to his willingness to accept me (symbolized by him embracing me).

It's important to understand that before he could present his vulnerabilities to anyone, he most assuredly had to accept them himself. Our vulnerabilities are part of who we are and however we choose to deal with them points to who we will become.

> *If the Good News we preach is hidden behind a veil, it is hidden only from people who are perishing. Satan, who is the god of this world, has blinded the minds of those who don't believe. They are unable to see the glorious light of the Good News. They don't understand this message about the glory of Christ, who is the exact likeness of God.*
>
> 2 Corinthians 4:3-4

Acceptance is key. It's crucial. The greatest mysteries of the universe are locked within us. The more we reject ourselves, the more we will reject others, thereby moving further from the truth of who we really are and staying in a cycle of rejection and relationship purgatory. Without acceptance, we drown repeatedly in a vast gulf of emptiness.

> **crucial**
> 1. *vital to the resolution of a crisis; decisive*
> 2. *extremely significant or important*
> 3. *of the form of a cross; cross-shaped*
>
>   (Dictionary.com, 2010)

Accepting who you were, allows you to embrace who you are, which gives you confidence to develop fully into the person you're becoming. With that confidence you can move forward by accepting others as they are, vulnerabilities and all.

I accept all of thee...

A couple of weekends after Thanksgiving, the focus scripture in my church service came from *Micah 5:1-6*. Verse four connected all the clues in this message for me: *He will stand and shepherd his flock in the strength of the LORD.*

The verse stood out for two reasons: 1) The solid stance of the man in my dream represented security and strength to me 2) Sanctus Real's song, *Lead Me*, had been looping in my mind for several weeks prior and I couldn't figure out what it was trying to tell me. The lyrics are a beautiful blend of a man's strength and vulnerability through his multiple roles and responsibilities. The refrain is written from a wife's and child's perspective:

> *Lead me with strong hands*
> *Stand up when I can't*
> *Don't leave me hungry for love*
> *Chasing dreams, what about us?*
> *Show me you're willing to fight*
> *That I'm still the love of your life*
> *I know we call this our home*
> *But I still feel alone*
>
> (Hammitt, 2010)

The song is a prayer for God to lead the man – the husband, the father – to be the strength of his family – the provider, comforter and defender – through *God's* grace and power, not his own. He couldn't possibly do it on his own. It's a moving prayer of a man asking for the strength to love his family through his presence and with the best offerings of his life.

It's such a vulnerable plea, and for that reason, there is so much power in it.

The convergence of all these elements had me analyzing aspects of my own life. Specifically, the lack of strong hands throughout my childhood and adulthood and the fact that there has never been anyone (father or other) standing or fighting for me. There has been no one willing to live and share with me. I marveled at the realization that my hunger for love had turned into such a state of starvation that I've perhaps ceased to feel. Wonder of wonders, I wondered how different my life would be had I been blessed with a father who lead rather than destroyed?

It all rolls up to love. The best expression, the most lasting impression of love that we will receive in this life is through our father, mother, and spouse (husband or wife). If they aren't led by the spirit of God, His love for us will not be experienced through them and we could remain hungry for love, chasing useless things in a lonely life because we have no idea how to *be* representatives of love or how to *receive* love as vessels.

Fortunately, the sad, lonely low points of neglect and uncertainty puts us in a special space for grace. I thank God for my vulnerabilities and my willingness to accept and embrace them. The more vulnerable I am, the stronger God's presence in my life becomes. The same grace is available to you.

> *Three times I pleaded with the Lord to take it away from me. But He said to me, "My grace is sufficient for you, for my power is made perfect in weakness." Therefore I will boast all the more gladly about my weaknesses, so that Christ's power may rest on me. That is why, for Christ's sake, I delight in weaknesses, in insults, in hardships, in persecutions, in difficulties. For when I am weak, then I am strong.*
>
> *~ 2 Corinthians 12:8-10*

It's all about me (not really)...

I want to be accepted unconditionally as I am. I want to be loved fully as a product of God. I want to repent without judgment, punishment or condemnation. I want forgiveness that evolves me as an individual and as a partner in my relationships.

It's all about you (yeah, right)...

You're no different from me. Our desires are the same. You want full acceptance for the person you are now. You want to be loved without conditions. You want to make your relationships right. You want to repent with the assurance that your relationships will improve with your show of vulnerability. You want to forgive as much as you want to be forgiven.

Truly, in all honesty, it's all about God!

It's always been about God. Not only how visible and palpable He is in our lives, but how ACTIVE He is IN us. Are we allowing God to be God or are we limiting Him by insisting we be who we want to be (and/or insisting others be as we want them to be)?

Mary and Joseph learned this lesson as harshly as any parent could. Jesus was their son. Even though they knew the calling on His life and the purpose for it, He was still their little boy and they expected Him to act as such while in their care. But there were times when God's plan trumped their assignment. For example, we're told in Luke 2 that Mary and Joseph took their annual family trip to Jerusalem for the Passover festival. After the festival, they headed home with a caravan of fellow travelers. It was some time before they realized twelve-year-old Jesus was not with their group.

> When they couldn't find him, they went back to Jerusalem to search for him there. Three days later they finally discovered him in the Temple, sitting among the religious teachers, listening to them and asking questions. All who heard him were amazed at his understanding and his answers.
>
> His parents didn't know what to think. "Son," his mother said to him, "why have you done this to us?

> *Your father and I have been frantic, searching for you everywhere."*
>
> *"But why did you need to search?" he asked. "Didn't you know that I must be in my Father's house?"*
>
> *Jesus grew in wisdom and in stature and in favor with God and all the people.*
>
> *~ Luke 2:41-49, 52*

We limit God in our lives when we persist in holding on to our nature – our fleshly desires (not necessarily sexual, but anything that is against what God wants for us at any given point of our life). God does not transform us in the flesh, He transforms our hearts through our spiritual relationship with Him. That transformation manifests in our physical life.

> *"Therefore, give the people of Israel this message from the Sovereign LORD: I am bringing you back, but not because you deserve it. I am doing it to protect My holy name, on which you brought shame while you were scattered among the nations. I will show how holy My great name is — the name on which you brought shame among the nations. And when I reveal My holiness through you before their very eyes, says the Sovereign LORD, then the nations will know that I am the LORD. For I will gather you up from all the nations and bring you home again to your land.*
>
> *"Then I will sprinkle clean water on you, and you will be clean. Your filth will be washed away, and you will no longer worship idols. And I will give you a new heart, and I will put a new spirit in you. I will take out your stony, stubborn heart and give you a tender, responsive heart. And I will put my Spirit in you so that you will follow my decrees and be careful to obey my regulations.*
>
> *~ Ezekiel 36:22-27*

In order to allow God to be God in our lives (I.e. Lord of our life), we *must* SURRENDER EVERYTHING about ourselves to the control and guidance of His Holy Spirit. When the Holy Spirit is in control of our lives we become ripe, populating fruit eager to give and receive love. Quick to repent and accept repentance from those who offend us. Humble in asking for forgiveness and merciful in giving it.

> *May God, who gives this patience and encouragement, help you live in complete harmony with each other, as is fitting for followers of Christ Jesus. Then all of you can join together with one voice, giving praise and glory to God, the Father of our Lord Jesus Christ.*
> *~ Romans 15:5-6*

Dear Reader:

Know that you are loved with a supernatural love that never diminishes or fails. In fact, it multiplies with use; the more you share it, the more it grows. Your best example of repentance is Christ's obedience on the cross; His willingness to sacrifice himself to fulfill God's purpose for His life and for mankind. The grace of God's unilateral forgiveness is the reward for all the suffering that has come before.

Walk forward in love and the blessings in your life will overflow into the lives of others.

> *"I will make you into a great nation, and I will bless you; I will make your name great, and you will be a blessing."*
>
> *~ Genesis 12:2*

Scripture Index

Belief	John 1:10-12	13
Belief	Hebrews 11:6	14
Belief	John 20:31	14
Belief	Romans 10:9-10	15
Belief	Romans 10:9-13	15
Belief	1 John 4:1-3	19
Belief	2 Corinthians 6:14	37
Belief	Psalm 31:14-15	46
Belief	Acts 2:1-4	48
Belief	Luke 8:5-8	53
Belief	Luke 8:11-15	54
Belief	Matthew 13:57-58	62
Belief	2 Corinthians 4:3-4	190
Communication	Jeremiah 1:12	29
Communication	Proverbs 16:24	140
Communication	Proverbs 24:26	143
Communication	Psalm 119:103	144
Communication	Matthew 7:7-11	146
Communication	Genesis 11:6-7	149, 150
Communication	Genesis 11:1-9	151
Communication	Matthew 18:19-20	152
Communication	Psalm 55:21	154
Communication	Genesis 3:8-9	158
Communication	John 16:24	176
Faith	Hebrews 11:1	14
Faith	Hebrews 11:6	14
Faith	Philippians 3:12-14	28
Faith	Jeremiah 1:12	29
Faith	Jude 1:20-21	101
Faith	Jude 1:22-23	136

Faith	*Matthew 21:21-22*	147
Faith	*John 16:20-24*	161
Faith	*1 Samuel 30:6*	163
Faith	*1 John 4:1*	163
Faith	*Proverbs 4:7*	163
Forgiveness	*Hebrews 10:19-22*	65
Forgiveness	*2 Samuel 12:1-14*	79
Forgiveness	*Psalm 32:1-5*	84
Forgiveness	*Psalm 32:1*	89
Forgiveness	*Psalm 32:1-2*	89
Forgiveness	*Matthew 10:31-32*	98
Forgiveness	*Matthew 6:14-15*	108, 109
Forgiveness	*John 20:21-23*	109
Forgiveness	*Matthew 6:9-13*	110
Forgiveness	*Matthew 18:21-35*	111
Forgiveness	*1 John 2:12*	116
Forgiveness	*Matthew 16:19*	117
Forgiveness	*John 20:21-23*	117
Forgiveness	*Matthew 18:15-17*	119
Forgiveness	*2 Samuel 12:7-10*	121
Forgiveness	*Matthew 18:21-22*	123
Forgiveness	*Acts 7:59-60*	127
Forgiveness	*Luke 23:34*	127
Forgiveness	*Matthew 18:18*	128
Forgiveness	*Matthew 5:23-24*	130
Forgiveness	*Isaiah 43:24-26*	138
Forgiveness	*Isaiah 1:18-20*	139
Forgiveness	*Luke 6:37-38*	174
Forgiveness	*1 John 1:7-10*	178
Forgiveness	*1 John 2:1-2*	180
Forgiveness	*Colossians 1:19-22*	187
Forgiveness	*Psalm 51:10-12*	187
Forgiveness	*Ezekiel 36:22-27*	194
Honor God	*1 Corinthians 6:19*	41, 48
Honor God	*1 Corinthians 10:31-33*	41
Honor God	*Romans 12:12*	41
Honor God	*Proverbs 3:9-10*	47
Honor God	*Malachi 3:10*	47, 48
Honor God	*1 Corinthians 15:20*	48, 53
Honor God	*John 4:23-24*	48

Honor God	Malachi 3:8-11	48
Honor God	Psalm 24:1	49
Honor God	John 4:23-24	49
Honor God	Mark 12:15-17	49
Honor God	Romans 12:1	51
Honor God	Romans 14:1-8	52
Honor God	Matthew 25:24	55
Honor God	Leviticus 11:44	64
Honor God	Matthew 25:40	125
Honor God	Galatians 5:16:18	125
Honor God	Galatians 5:16-18	132
Honor God	Mark 10:14-16	143
Honor God	Matthew 16:13-17	154
Honor God	Deuteronomy 4:16-20	166
Honor God	2 Corinthians 11:3	167
Honor God	Proverbs 27:23	177
Honor God	1 John 2:3-6	180
Honor God	Romans 15:7	183
Honor God	Romans 15:16	183
Honor God	John 14:6-7	186
Honor God	2 Corinthians 12:8-10	192
Honor God	Luke 2:41-49	193
Honor God	Ezekiel 36:22-27	194
Honor God	Luke 2:52	194
Honor God	Romans 15:5-6	195
Identity	1 Peter 2:9	11
Identity	1 Peter 2:11-12	11
Identity	John 1:10-12	13
Identity	1 John 4:1-3	19
Identity	Jeremiah 1:5	24
Identity	Jeremiah 29:11	25
Identity	Psalm 91	25
Identity	2 Corinthians 6:14	37
Identity	2 Corinthians 5:18-21	38
Identity	2 Corinthians 4:6	39
Identity	2 Corinthians 5:20	40
Identity	Revelation 3:16	45
Identity	Matthew 7:19-20	63
Identity	Leviticus 11:44	64
Identity	Exodus 34:12	92
Identity	Exodus 34:14	92

Identity	*Galatians 5:1*	*131*
Identity	*Galatians, 5:13-15*	*131*
Identity	*Romans 12:3-5*	*168*
Identity	*Romans 2:29*	*171*
Identity	*Romans 12:2*	*171*
Identity	*Romans 11:35-36*	*174*
Identity	*John 1:1-5*	*175*
Identity	*Romans 11:36*	*175*
Identity	*2 Corinthians 5:16-17*	*181*
Identity	*Romans 15:7*	*183*
Identity	*1 John 4:16-18*	*184*
Identity	*1 John 4:20-21*	*185*
Identity	*Colossians 1:19-22*	*187*
Identity	*Micah 5:4*	*188*
Identity	*Micah 5:1-6*	*190*
Identity	*2 Corinthians 4:3-4*	*190*
Identity	*Luke 2:41-49*	*193*
Identity	*Genesis 12:2*	*196*
Life & Death	*Deuteronomy 30:19-20*	*44*
Life & Death	*Matthew 4:4*	*48*
Life & Death	*Acts 17:28*	*60*
Life & Death	*1 John 3:14-15*	*75*
Life & Death	*Ezekiel 18:30-32*	*85*
Life & Death	*Romans 6:20-23*	*90*
Life & Death	*Romans 6:20-21*	*93*
Life & Death	*Romans 6:22-23*	*93*
Life & Death	*1 Corinthians 15:21-22*	*95*
Life & Death	*Deuteronomy 30:15-20*	*113*
Life & Death	*Genesis 2:9*	*115*
Life & Death	*Genesis 2:16-17*	*115*
Love	*Matthew 22:37-40*	*18*
Love	*Isaiah 30:18*	*21*
Love	*1 John 4:7-8*	*22*
Love	*1 Corinthians 13:4-7*	*23*
Love	*Galatians 5:22-23*	*26*
Love	*1 John 3:18-19*	*28*
Love	*Hosea 3:1*	*28*
Love	*1 John 4:19*	*29*
Love	*1 John 4:17-18*	*31*
Love	*John 14:21*	*31*

Love	1 Corinthians 13:12-13	32
Love	1 Peter 4:8	33
Love	John 15:12-13	34
Love	John 3:16	35, 41, 52
Love	John 3:17	36
Love	1 John 4:9-12	37
Love	Proverbs 27:5	37
Love	1 John 4:16	38
Love	Matthew 10:5-8	41
Love	John 15:13-14	42
Love	Ephesians 5:28-29	43
Love	John 15:13	43
Love	1 John 4:18-19	45
Love	I Corinthians 13:4-8	45
Love	Romans 5:5	49
Love	Galatians 5:22-23	50
Love	Philemon 1:6-7	56
Love	1 Peter 4:8	57, 65
Love	Song of Solomon 8:6	60
Love	Romans 8:35	61
Love	Romans 8:37-39	61
Love	1 John 3:14-15	75
Love	1 Corinthians 13:7	76
Love	Psalm 51:1	76
Love	1 Corinthians 13:5	77
Love	1 Corinthians 13:6	78
Love	1 Corinthians 8:1-3	100
Love	Jude 1:20-21	101
Love	Matthew 6:9-13	110
Love	1 John 4:9-11	116
Love	Proverbs 14:30	119
Love	Hebrews 12:15	128
Love	Galatians 5:1	131
Love	Galatians, 5:13-15	131
Love	John 14:15	131
Love	Matthew 22:37-39	131
Love	Galatians 5:22-26	133
Love	Jude 1:22-23	136
Love	Jude 1:2	137
Love	Proverbs 16:24	140
Love	Luke 6:37-38	174
Love	Proverbs 11:24-25	176

Love	Proverbs 27:23	177
Love	1 John 4:16-18	184
Love	1 John 4:20-21	185
Love	John 14:6-7	186
Repentance	2 Peter 3:9-10	12
Repentance	Luke 3:8	68
Repentance	2 Corinthians 7:11	69
Repentance	2 Corinthians 7:9-12	70
Repentance	Psalm 51	72
Repentance	1 John 1:8-10	74
Repentance	Psalm 51:1	76
Repentance	Psalm 51:9	76
Repentance	Psalm 51:12-13	77
Repentance	Psalm 51:17	78
Repentance	2 Samuel 12:1-14	79
Repentance	Acts 2:38-39	82
Repentance	Proverbs 28:13-14	82
Repentance	Psalm 32:1-5	84
Repentance	Ezekiel 18:30-32	85
Repentance	Luke 3:8-9	85
Repentance	Proverbs 28:13	87
Repentance	Psalm 32:3-4	87
Repentance	Psalm 51:16-17	88
Repentance	Romans 6:20-23	90
Repentance	Romans 6:20-21	93
Repentance	Romans 6:22-23	93
Repentance	Ezekiel 18:3-4	94
Repentance	Ezekiel 18:30-32	94, 95
Repentance	Psalm 36:1-4	97
Repentance	2 Corinthians 7:8-13	102
Repentance	2 Samuel 12:7-10	121
Repentance	Psalm 51:17	129
Repentance	Matthew 5:23-24	130
Security	Psalm 4:8	24
Security	Psalm 91	25
Security	Galatians 5:1	52

NOTES

NOTES

NOTES

NOTES

Works Cited

Dictionary, T. F. (n.d.). *The Free Dictionary*. Retrieved 12 2010, from http://www.thefreedictionary.com

Dictionary.com. (2010). *Dictionary.com*. Retrieved November 15, 2010, from Dictionary.com: http://dictionary.reference.com/

Hammitt, M. (Composer). (2010). Lead Me. [Sanctus Real, Performer] USA.

Jones, L. (2009). *My God and Me: Listening, Learning and Growing on My Journey.* New York: Jazzy Media LLC.

Leland Ryken, J. W. (1998). *Dictionary of Biblical Imagery.* Downers Grove, IL: InterVarsity Press, USA.

Meyer, J. (1994). *Beauty for Ashes.* New York: Warner Books.

Mick Jones, L. G. (Composer). (1984). I Want to Know What Love Is. [Foreigner, Performer, & M. Jones, Conductor] United Kingdom.

Reiner, R. (Director). (1992). *A Few Good Men* [Motion Picture].

The Burnaby and Mission SDA Churches. (n.d.). Retrieved November 2, 2010, from The Gospel Herald: http://www.gospel-herald.com/faith_and_works.htm

Yoonu Njub (radio program). (1998). *Cain and Abel: The Way of Sacrifice.* Retrieved October 28, 2010, from The Way of Righteousness: Good News for Muslims.

VISIT MYGODANDME.INFO

Additional Work by LaShawnda Jones

My God and Me
Listening, Learning and Growing on My Journey

mygodandme.info

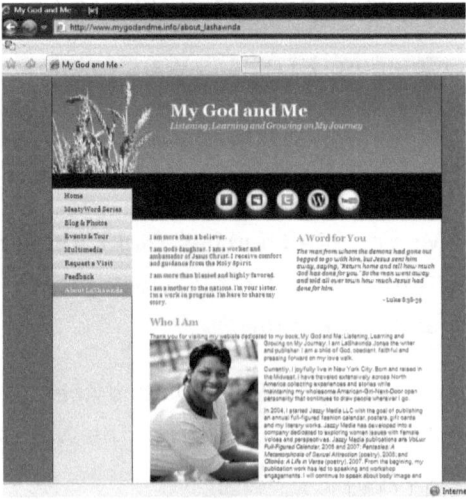

VISIT MYGODANDM.INFO

About the Author

LaShawnda Jones is currently living and thriving in New York City. Her writing and publishing work range from developing volumes of poetry to designing an annual full-figured calendar. She also contributed to a daily political blog during the 2008 presidential election and an anthology of letters addressed to First Lady Michelle Obama.

LaShawnda's life is an illustration of transition – constant movement and growth from one point to another. She is ecstatic about continuing forward on her journey with the LORD. She continues to grow stronger in her faith, wiser in her knowledge and more loving to people as she seeks to mirror exactly the Christ in her.

To keep up with LaShawnda's journey, subscribe to her blog at www.mygodandme.info/blog.

www.ingramcontent.com/pod-product-compliance
Lightning Source LLC
Chambersburg PA
CBHW031245290426
44109CB00012B/448